John Millar

Letters of Crito

On the Causes, Objects, and Consequences of the Present War

John Millar

Letters of Crito
On the Causes, Objects, and Consequences of the Present War

ISBN/EAN: 9783337138189

Printed in Europe, USA, Canada, Australia, Japan

Cover: Foto ©Suzi / pixelio.de

More available books at **www.hansebooks.com**

LETTERS

OF

CRITO,

ON THE

CAUSES, OBJECTS, AND CONSEQUENCES,

OF THE

PRESENT WAR.

Quo, quo scelesti, ruitis?————
————Furorne cæcos, an rapit vis acrior,
An culpa? responsum date.　　　　Hor.

LONDON:

Printed for and fold by J. Debrett, oppofite to Burlington-
houfe, Piccadilly; J. Johnson, St. Paul's Church-
yard; and G. G. and J. Robinsons,
Paternofter-Row.

———

1796.

T. IV. 21.

No perfon of reflection can perufe the following Letters, without obferving that the details which they contain are a compleat fulfilment of the memorable prediction uttered by Mr. Fox, in the Houfe of Commons, near four years ago.

Honeft and candid men, of all parties, now willingly avow their conviction, that, if the advice which that great Statefman then gave in his place, had been feafonably followed by his Majefty's Minifters, Great Britain would have acquired a degree of profperity, of opulence and power, and a rank and dignity of character among the Nations of Europe, far fuperior to what fhe ever poffeffed during the moft fplendid periods of her former hiftory.

From the confequences of meafures adopted in oppofition to that advice, and perfifted in with criminal and incorrigible obftinacy, good men wifh it were poffible for them to turn away their eyes.—One hundred millions of the National Treafure already fquandered,—from thirty to forty millions more to be immediately raifed,—and the total enormous amount loft to this country for ever.—Taxes nearly doubled.—Millions of human lives barbaroufly facrificed.—Many thoufands of families reduced, from fituations of independence and high refpectability, to beggary and wretchednefs.—The national character degraded, derided, or execrated abroad;—the conftitution attacked and ftabbed in its vitals at home.—Thefe are fome of the mifchiefs that have arifen out of the mad profecution of this WAR of MINISTERS.

To you, ye authors, and abettors, of all this wanton ha-
vock and defolation of your country, and of the human race,
may an humble individual be permitted to addrefs a well-
meant admonition, in the words of SHAKESPEARE :—

———Confefs yourfelves to Heaven ;
Repent what's paft—AVOID WHAT IS TO COME;
And do not fpread the compoft on the weeds,
To make them ranker.—Forgive me this my virtue ;
For, in the fatnefs of thefe purfy times,
Virtue itfelf of Vice muft pardon beg,
Yea courb, and woo for leave to do it good.

CHARLES JAMES FOX.

SIR,

THE Author of the following publication entertains the perfuafion, in common with all thinking and impartial people, that the plan of policy which you recommended to Minifters, in the moft forcible terms, at the opening of the feffion of parliament towards the clofe of 1792, would, if then adopted, have enfured the permanence of our national profperity, while it would have preferved all Europe from the calamities which it has fince endured.

He is likewife perfuaded, as all thinking and impartial people are, that until fuch time as His Majefty, in his royal wifdom, and paternal affection for his People, fhall be gracioufly pleafed to difmifs from his prefence and councils thofe Minifters whofe pernicious meafures have produced our prefent cala-

mities, no reafonable hope can be entertained of the eftablifhment of a Peace
fuitable to the interefts of Great Britain,
and likely to preferve the tranquillity
of Europe.

Having thus far explained the fentiments of the Author, I flatter myfelf
you will have the goodnefs to acquit
me of the guilt of prefumption in wifhing to draw your attention to the Letters of Crito.

I have the honour to be,

Sir,

Your moft obedient

And moft faithful humble fervant,

THE EDITOR.

PREFACE.

AS the Editor of the Scots Chronicle has thought proper to collect and re-publish the following Letters, which first appeared in his Miscellany, the Author cannot help feeling, at their appearance in a separate publication, a degree of uneasiness, of which he was not sensible when they lay scattered among the other materials of a Newspaper. He hoped that the manner of publication, in the one case, might afford some apology, which will be wanting, and which, he fears, will be much needed in the other. As the Letters were written occasionally, at different periods, he is apprehensive that they may contain, on the one hand, numerous repetitions; and on the other, may be too desultory, to exhibit a connected view of the several particulars which he meant to convey. His intention was, in the first place, to throw together some remarks upon the origin and progress of *those political changes which have lately taken place in France; and to examine how far the conduct of the people, in that country, together with the system of government which they have at length established, has proceeded from their own free choice, and how far it has been influenced and varied by the jealousy, and the hostile interposition of neighbouring nations.—This naturally led him to consider the conduct of the other states of Europe, who formed, and carried into execution, a regular plan for preventing, by force, the French people from modelling their own government according to their own will.*

Of all the European states, it may seem surprising that Britain should have felt the greatest disturbance from the French Revolution, and have made the most violent exertions for preventing its completion. The mildest, and the most limited monarchy in the world has affected the greatest apprehension, lest the example of a political change, in a neighbouring country, should shake the foundations of her authority. It is the purpose of these Letters to point out the causes of this extraordinary phenomenon;

to explain the true motives by which our Mi-
niſtry were induced to enter into a war with
France ; to aſcertain the real objeĉt of that
war, in contradiſtinĉtion to thoſe plauſible pre-
tences which they aſſumed in order to conceal
their deſigns ; and thence to diſcover the grounds
of their obſtinacy in proſecuting this unfortunate
conteſt, notwithſtanding many fair opportunities
which have been preſented for obtaining an ad-
vantageous peace. Theſe inquiries are conclud-
ed by ſome refleĉtions upon the injuſtice and the
impolicy of this miniſterial conduĉt ; upon the un-
fortunate ſituation into which it has reduced us ;
and upon the meaſures which, in our preſent
circumſtances, appear indiſpenſibly neceſſary.

It muſt be confeſſed, that the piĉture, which
is thus exhibited, of this great ſcene of Euro-
pean tranſaĉtions, is far from being a pleaſant
one ; and that the part which has been per-
formed by the Britiſh nation is not ſuch as
'll tend to gratify national vanity. Whether
it be a true piĉture, is, with due deference,
ſubmitted to the Public. The inhabitants of
this devoted country have too long negleĉted to
ſee with their own eyes ; and have placed too

*much confidence in men who have had an in-
terest to deceive them. They have, according-
ly, been made the dupes of an interested policy;
and have suffered themselves to be misled by a
train of artful and delusive representation. It
is now high time to examine the consequences
of their simplicity; and to behold the precipice
upon which they stand. The observations contained in the following Letters may, perhaps,
assist in this examination, and afford a clue to
unravel the mysterious designs of some of the
principal parties. Their publication, it is hoped, will not seem improper in this dangerous
crisis, and when we have so near a prospect of
the meeting of a new parliament. To this new
assembly, not embarassed or prejudiced by opinions declared in the former, the nation must
look, with eager expectation, for such interpo-
sitions as may alleviate our distress, and avert
the impending calamities.*

THE AUTHOR.

LETTER I.

TO THE EDITOR OF THE SCOTS CHRONICLE.

SIR,   May 27. 1796.

THE French Revolution, and the war in
which we have been involved on that account, are,
doubtlefs, the moft fingular events which have occurred in the courfe of the prefent century. The
abolition of the old government in France, and
the conftitution eftablifhed there in 1789, were
beheld, by men of enlarged views, with equal fur-
prife and fatisfaction. The real friends of liberty
were highly gratified by the fudden overthrow of
a defpotifm which had, for ages, been apparently
gathering folidity and firmnefs ; a defpotifm which,
in the progrefs of civilized manners, had acquired
the moft plaufible appearance of which, perhaps,
that fpecies of government is fufceptible ; and
they were no lefs delighted to fee, in its place, a
regular fyftem of limited monarchy reared, as by
the power of enchantment, and fitted, all at once,
for the immediate ufe and accommodation of the
people.

A

The poceedings, indeed, in relation to this great revolution, were in many refpects liable to exception. The changes introduced were not, in all cafes, juftified by neceffity. Though the old privileges, immunities, and peculiar jurifdiction of the clergy, and of the nobility, were with great propriety abolifhed, the entire abolition of the titles and rank of the latter appeared a needlefs and infolent ftretch of innovation. The frivolous minutenefs, too, of the leaders and directors of this great tranfaction, the affectation of philofophic accuracy with which they entered upon many ab-ftract and ufelefs queftions, and the pomp of fyfte-nratic regularity with which they endeavoured to exhibit and to adorn their new political fyftem, were difgufting to many, and were confidered rather as the juvenile efforts of raw and fpeculative politici-ans, than as the folid productions of experienced and profound ftatefmen. Upon the whole, how-ever, the new inftitution, with all the objections which could be made to it, and notwithftanding all the ridicule attempted to be thrown upon the perfons engaged in conducting it, appeared, in the eye of reafon, to be fraught with numberlefs ad-vantages to the French nation, and likely to pro-duce over all Europe, perhaps over the whole globe, a rich field of inftruction and example to the human race.

The peculiar circumftances which, by irritating and provoking the French people, and by creat-ing inextricable difficulties and embarraffment to administration, became the immediate occasion of breaking down the old goverment, have been clearly pointed out, and fully stated, in a late publication by a Noble Author of this country. Among these, the imprudent behaviour of some part of the Royal Family, the disgust excited by a glaring outrage to the military spirit of the nation, and the thoughtless profusion, which, promoted by the practice of funding, had led to a national bankruptcy, may perhaps be regarded as the most conspicuous. But the ultimate cause of this great phenomenon appears to be no other, than the general diffusion of knowledge, and the progress of science and philosophy.

Men are disposed to submit to goverment, either from the mere influence of *authority*, or from the prospect of the advantages to be derived from that submission. The former principle is the effect of an immediate feeling or instinct; it acquires additional strength from habit, and rises commonly to its highest pitch in the ages of ignorance and barbarism. The latter supposes information and reflection, and may be expected to become the prevailing principle, in proportion as the understanding is cultivated, and as reason triumphs over ancient prejudices.

Among all the great nations of Europe, the French were the first who attained that state of civilization which is necessary to encourage liberal pursuits; and as they have remained longer in that situation, their progress, in the natural course of

things, has been fo much the greater. In the
other countries upon the Continent, this point is
is undifputed. The French literature, tafte, and
fafhions, are univerfally confidered as a model for
imitation.

England, with its dependancies, appears alone
to difpute this univerfal fuperiority. In many
branches of philofophy, indeed, the Englifh have
certainly been eminently diflinguifhed; and we
might mention the names of a Newton, a Locke,
a Hume, and a Smith, with feveral others, which
will not eafily be matched by the neighbouring
nations. But in England, literature is a good deal
confined to men of learned profeffions; whereas in
France, the refult of the difcoveries of all feems
known to every perfon of education. A philofopher, in that country, is no peculiar character;
but correfponds to what we fhould call a gentleman. Every part of knowledge, even that which
is derived from the abftract fciences, enters into
common converfation, and is handled almoft equally by both fexes.

In England, too, it muft be admitted, that literature, even among perfons intended for the learned
profeffions, is narrow and frivolous: Inftead of purfuing an extenfive range of ufeful and ornamental
knowledge, what is called a learned man, is frequently occupied merely in fcanning Latin verfes,
and in acquiring a very minute acquaintance with
two dead languages. He reads even Latin and
Greek authors, not for the fake of the information

contained in them, but on account of the claffical purity of their compofitions; and a public fpeak-er often interlards his difcourfe with fcraps of La-tin fentences, in which the thought, if expreffed in his mother tongue, would feem unworthy of no-tice. The French are above this pedantry. Up-on the firft revival of letters, they were, like the Englifh, engroffed by objects of this nature; but according to the advancement of tafte and fcience, their views have been enlarged, and their purfuits rendered more manly. The knowledge, which has diffufed itfelf over all that part of the fociety exempted from bodily labour, could hardly fail to fhed its rays upon the fubject of government, and in that quarter, as well as in others, to en-lighten the great body of the people. It has en-abled them to examine, and to defpife the quackery of politicians, to explode the fuperftition of old inftitutions, and to render authority fubfervient to general utility. How far they have always rea-foned properly upon this fubject, I fhall not at pre-fent enquire. That they have ventured here to fpeculate boldly, and have fallen into errors, is of a piece with their conduct in regard to religion, and to other branches of fcience.

But whatever were the caufes of the French Revolution, the alarm and terror which it fpread in the neighbouring countries of Europe may be confidered as the moft natural, and the leaft fur-prifing of all its confequences. The confideration of this, however, would lead me too far at prefent.

If you think thefe hints worthy of infertion in fome corner of your well conducted Paper, you may poffibly be troubled with more of the fame fort. I am, &c.

CRITO.

LETTER II.

TO THE EDITOR OF THE SCOTS CHRONICLE.

SIR,   June 3. 1796.

THE French Revolution, which took place in 1789, was not hoftile to kingly government: It went no farther than to eftablifh a limited monarchy. The abufes in the ancient political fyftem were fo numerous, and had attained fuch magnitude, as to exclude every idea of a partial reform, and to require a complete and radical change. The king had acquired an abfolute power over the lives and fortunes of all his fubjects. He might throw them into prifon without affigning any caufe, and fubject them, at pleafure, to perpetual confinement. If the ordinary courts of juftice were not fufficiently obfequious, he might name other judges for trying any offence in the laft refort. He had an unlimited power of making laws and of impofing taxes. The nobility, though dependent upon the crown, had intereft to procure an exemption from the greater part of taxes; and they exercifed very arbitrary powers over their tenants and vaffals. The higher clergy were a fort of nobles, poffeffing enormous wealth, with fimilar powers and exemptions; while thofe of inferior rank were deprefled with poverty, and fubjected to the whole burden of the clerical functions.

When a reformation of political abufes is to be obtained with concurence of the exifting government, it is a maxim of common prudence, that it fhould proceed flowly and gradually, fo as not to endanger the public tranquillity, by counteracting old habits, and lofing all fight of the former uf-ages. But when a great change is to be extorted in oppofition to the conftituted authorities, it muft be effected all at once : the machine of adminiftra-tion muft be brought into the hands of the reform-ers; and precautions muft be taken for preventing the partizans of the old fyftem from producing a counter-revolution. This was the fituation in France. If the people, therefore, had been con-tented with lopping off a fmall branch from the power of the crown, the effect of their labours would have remained no longer than till the popu-lar enthufiafm had fubfided ; and their attempt would have ferved no other purpofe than to rivet their chains, and to draw upon them the vengeance of an irritated and jealous defpot. When a high-wayman demands your money, it is not enough, if we mean to make refiftance, that we fhould feize his piftol, and let him go ; for ten to one he has another in his pocket. We muft lay hold of him, and fecure his perfon; otherwife we had better not have provoked his refentment.

The leaders of the French people may, on this
account, be vindicated for endeavouring to new-
model their government; though they feem to
have aimed at a certain ideal perfection beyond
what, perhaps, is confiftent with the conduct of
human affairs. Their great object was to commit
the fupreme power to a national affembly, compof-
ed of reprefentatives, not nominal and fictitious as
is in fome other countries, but really chofen by the
nation at large. For this purpofe, all the male
inhabitants of different diftricts, with very few
exceptions, were empowered to choofe electors for
larger departments; and thefe laft nominated the
members of the national affembly.

A confiderable fhare of the executive power
was, at the fame time, devolved upon the king,
who had, befides, a negative upon the determina-
tions of the legiflature; a negative, which was not
merely a fhadow, but was intended to be commonly exercifed. The king was likewife invefted with
no inconfiderable patronage; and the civil lift,
entirely at his difpofal, amounted, in our money,
nearly to a million and a half. The influence and
power of the crown were thus, in fome refpects,
greater than in this ifland.

It is a difficult to form a decided opinion concerning the merits of any fyftem of government,
before it has been actually proved by experiment;
but this, as far as mere fpeculation can enable us
to determine, has the appearance of a liberal
fyftem, greatly fuperior to moft of thofe which

have ever been eftablifhed in a great nation. As
to the double election of the national reprefentatives, it feems peculiarly calculated for fecuring an
equal reprefentation; and in that view it is highly
approved of by two eminent writers, Harrington
and Hume, the latter of whom was far from being
a favourer of popular licence.

In proportion as the French Revolution was
grateful to thofe who rejoiced in the extenfion of
political liberty, it gave rife to very unpleafant
fenfations in the abfolute fovereigns of Europe.
Their authority was obvioufly founded upon opinion; and that opinion refted upon old cuftom
and prejudice. If the people fhould once be led
to *think* upon the fubject of government, they
muft immediately fee the abfurdity of facrificing
their lives, and every thing they hold valuable, to
the private intereft, to the avarice and ambition, to
the whim and caprice of a fingle individual. They
muft immediately fee that government is intended,
by the wife and good Author of nature, for the
benefit of the whole community; and that every
power, inconfiftent with this great principle, affumed by any perfon, under whatever title, of prince,
king, or emperor, is manifeftly unjuft and tyranni-
cal. There was every reafon to apprehend, that the
difpofition, which had now grown to fuch a height
in France, of prying into thefe matters of ftate, of
inveftigating principles which had long lain dor-
mant in the venerable lap of antiquity, would tear

off the covering from numberlefs ufurpations, and
produce a reformation of many enormous abufes.

How this revolution was, from the beginning,
viewed in England, it feems a matter of curiofity
to examine. I am, &c.

CRITO.

LETTER III.

TO THE EDITOR OF THE SCOTS CHRONICLE.

SIR,　　　　　　　　　　　June 7. 1796.

WHILE the French Revolution had become
the objeƈt of fuch alarm and terror in the neighbouring defpotical governments, it was regarded, by
many people in Britain, in a light lefs favourable
than might have been expeƈted. Inſtead of re-
joicing in the converſion of their ancient political
adverſaries to the principles of liberty, a confiderable part of the Englifh nation appears to have
viewed the tranfaƈtions in France with an eye of
jealoufy and difguſt. With all the folid good qua-
lities by which John Bull is diftinguifhed, it muſt
be confeffed, that he is not a little overrun with
prejudices. In the fimplicity of his heart, he is
apt to feel, and even to exprefs a blind prepoffeffion in favour of thofe ufages which have long
been familiar to him, and an overweening conceit
of himfelf on account of thofe advantages which
he has been fuppofed to enjoy. As the French
were accuftomed to prefcribe to their neighbours
with refpeƈt to the fafhions of drefs, and the modes

of ordinary behaviour; fo the Englifh have long claimed a fuperiority in politics, and have confidered their conftitution as a model of perfection. It could not fail, ·therefore, to fhock the feelings of many worthy politicians in England, to obferve that the French had the audacity to think for themfelves on that fubject; and that the Conftitution arifing from their united labours, differed, in many important particulars, from that which has been fo long eftablifhed and admired in this country.

This objection to the proceedings in France had probably lurked in the bofoms of more people than were willing to acknowledge it; but it foon came to be followed by another, which was thought of greater importance, and which produced a much greater effect upon perfons at the helm. The progrefs of knowledge, which, from the circumftances of fociety in England as well as in France, had pervaded a great proportion of the inhabitants, could not be prevented from exciting the fame fpirit of inquiry, and from producing a fimilar enlargement of ideas. Though the Englifh may be under ftrong prepoffeffions in fome points, their underftandings have been much exercifed on the fubject of politics. They have been long accuftomed to canvafs the meafures of adminiftration, to mark the line of conduct purfued by oppofition, and to examine the various topics which make the ground of contention and altercation between thofe two parties. Having a good

government, they are not difpofed to find fault
with it; but on the contrary, are impreffed with
a powerful bias towards all their own inftitutions
and cuftoms. Whatever may be thought of this
in philofophy, it certainly is a happy circumftance
in conduct; as it tends to difcourage ufelefs innovation and to avert thofe evils with which all violent changes in government are apt to be attended. But, notwithftanding this laudable difpofition
in the people, they could not fail to obferve the
urgent neceffity of correcting fome very flagrant
abufes, which, in the courfe of time, have crept
into our political fyftem, and which have, at length,
produced a remarkable deviation from its original
principles.

Of thefe, the Conftitution of the Houfe of Commons affords a glaring inftance. The advantages
of our mixed form of government, for preventing
the exceffes, either of pure monarchy, of arifto-
cracy, or of democracy, have been univerfally admitted; but in order to preferve the democratical
part, it is indifpenfably neceffary that the Houfe
of Commons fhould comprehend the reprefentatives of, at leaft, a confiderable proportion of the
whole nation. That this was the aim of our forefathers, in the formation of that Houfe, none but
ARTHUR YOUNG, the late *political* traveller, has
ever, fo far as I can obferve, been hardy enough
to difpute. But fo widely has the practice devi-
ated from the original principles of the Conftitution, that more than a majority of the Commons,

according to a late publication, are now in reality nominated, or returned by the intereſt of ſingle individuals ; and of theſe *real conſtituents*, it is likewiſe.to be obſerved, that a great proportion are peers, who, having a ſeat in the Upper Houſe, ought to have no ſhare in forming this other branch of the Legiſlature.

The neceſſity of a reform in this particular, to check the rapid advances of prerogative, and to retain the Conſtitution upon its ancient baſis, has long been acknowledged ; and a motion for this purpoſe, by men of great eminence and abilities, has repeatedly, though hitherto unſucceſsfully, been brought into parliament. The important tranſactions in France naturally recalled the attention of Britiſh ſubjects to the ſtate of their government at home ; and as the prevalence of greater abuſes in that neighbouring kingdom had produced a violent change of ſyſtem, it was thought by many, that in Britian we might thence derive an uſeful leſſon ; to correct, without loſs of time, the abuſes of our own Conſtitution ; to remove, by the ordinary and regular interpoſition of the Legiſlature, ſuch defects as had given any juſt ground of complaint ; and thus, by ſmall and partial alterations, to guard ourſelves from the danger of a total revolution. The greater the apprehenſions entertained from the example ſet before us, theſe precautions become the more indiſpenſible. If our neighbour is likely to ſuffer by a violent quack-medicine, we ſhould be the more anxious, in our

B

own cafe, to call an experienced and approved
phyſician ; and, if we are afraid of contagion from
abroad, we ſhould double our diligence in the
timely application of a remedy, which may prevent a ſlight diſtemper from being converted into
a deſperate diſeaſe.

The oppoſition, however, that has been made,
from intereſted motives, to a parliamentary reform,
and conſequently to the French Revolution, I ſhall .
afterwards take the liberty of conſidering.

I am, &c.

CRITO.

LETTER IV. .

TO THE EDITOR OF THE SCOTS CHRONICLE.

SIR,   June 10. 1796.

In my laſt letter, I hinted that, how rea-
ſonable or neceſſary ſoever a reform of the parliamentary repreſentation may appear, it is likely,
from views of private intereſt or ambition, to be,
on every occaſion, warmly and uniformly oppoſed
by many powerful individuals, and bodies of men.
This obſervation is chiefly applicable to perſons of
three different deſcriptions.

Men of great fortunes, the nobility and gentry,
who have acquired the nomination of members of
parliament, and who by that means are enabled to
gratify their ambition, and to promote their own
emolument, or that of their reſpective families,

have a great intereft, in retaining the prefent cor-
rupted fyftem, and may be fuppofed ready to employ every pretext whatever for warding off the
intended reformation.

I fhall not take upon me to cenfure, with immoderate feverity, the behaviour of fuch perfons.
They have a great pecuniary intereft at ftake. The
fums which have been given for, what is called,
the *property of a borough*, are immenfe. The
perfon who commands four or five of thefe boroughs is, befides, exalted to fuperior confideration
and rank. He is poffefled of a confiderable fhare
in the Legiflature of a great nation ; and may be
faid, in fome fort, to belong to a company of fovereign princes. When he ftruggles, therefore, to retain thofe advantages, at the expence of our national freedom, he only declines a facrifice which
few people would be willing to make. He cannot indeed fay, with the Apothecary in Shake-
fpeare, " My poverty, and not my will, con-
fents." But wealth, as well as poverty, has her ne-
ceffities ; at leaft her violent paffions, which produce no lefs powerful temptations. The misfortuue
is, that fuch perfons are, from their fituation, obliged to have the words, *public fpirit*, very frequently in their mouths. In a cafe of this nature,
to mention the fact will be fufficient ; I leave it
to the clergy, thofe efpecially in the fouthern part
of the ifland, who, from their profeffion, no doubt,
are abundantly difpofed to point out the immor-
ality of fuch conduct.

B ij

The rotten boroughs, themfelves, form another clafs, highly interefted to maintain the prefent
fyftem of corruption. Thefe, in their public capacity, will always be ftrongly actuated by a cor-
poration fpirit, and confidered as made up of individuals, educated in the detail of gainful profeffions, which lead them to reckon any thing according to the price that it will bring, are difpofed, of courfe, to weigh their privileges in the common fcale of mercantile profit. As an appendage
to thefe boroughs, may be confidered a multitude
of needy adventurers, who, having been unfuccefs-
ful in trade, and hoping to procure places or pen-
fions from government, derive an immediate benefit from that fyftem of things, which enables them
to fell their paltry fervices to the beft advantage.
To this clafs, alfo, may be joined the numerous
tribe of borough-mongers, thofe pimps and pand-
ers of political proftitution, who carry on a regular and lucrative trade by the infamous management of elections. All fuch people may be expected to unite as one man, in the practice of every
artifice within the fphere of their education and
abilities, for preventing a change that would re-
duce them to a ftate of beggary or infignificance.

The miniftry form a third clafs, more powerful
than the two former, and no lefs interefted in pre-
ferving thofe abufes, which put it in their power
fo eafily to overrule elections, and fo effectually to
defeat all the efforts of oppofition. To give a
hiftory of the conduct and fentiments of our Prime

Minifter, from his firft appearance on the political theatre, would be to probe an empoifoned fore, which, I am perfuaded, no ordinary medicine can cure. The popular arts by which he firft brought himfelf into notice ; his invectives againft the authors of the American war, and the zeal which he expreffed in promoting a reform of the reprefentation in parliament ; his arrogant, but veiy intelligible declaration, that he could not pretend to the firft minifterial fituation, and would not accept of a fecondary one ; his procuring that unconftitutional interference of the Crown in the deliberations of a great affembly, by which he forced himfelf into office ; and the long train of diffimulation and deception, which he practifed and *advifed*, for the purpofe of concealing the meafure of a diffolution of parliament that, in order to obtain a majority in the Houfe of Commons, he had all along determined to execute ; thefe are events, which, taken in connection with each other, will not foon be forgotten ; and, when compared with his pofterior conduct, they muft make an impreffion on the public mind which will not foon be effaced. That fuch a minifter, and his adherents, of fimilar principles, will not willingly relinquifh any part of the undue influence acquired by the crown, there is every reafon to believe.

How extenfive, at the fame time, this influence has become, and how univerfally it pervades all ranks and orders in the community, the army, the church, the retainers of the law, and of the revenue, thofe who fpeculate in monied and mercantile tranfactions; the nobility, the great corporations throughout the kingdom, not to mention placemen and penfioners, and the various claffes of executive officers; whoever examines the ftate of the fact, and confiders the vaft and increafing magnitude of the patronage, in the hands of adminiftration, will be at no lofs to difcover.

It is not furprifing, therefore, that when, in May 1792, a motion for obtaining a reform of the national reprefentation was made in the Houfe of Commons, by a gentleman no lefs diftinguifhed by his eloquence and fpirit, than by opulent family connections, which afford a pledge of his averfion to anarchy and popular difturbance, it excited uncommon marks of apprehenfion and terror. The meafure, though it had formerly been propofed by the minifter himfelf, was now reprefented as taking its orgin from the French Revolution; and as calculated to introduce in this country fimilar innovations to thofe which had taken place in France. To promote the fame idea, a royal proclamation was iffued foon after, tending to fpread an alarm over the country, and to infinuate fufpicions, that our happy conftitution was in danger from the propagation of, what are called, French opinions.

I am, &c.

CRITO.

LETTER V.

" Bella per Ematheos plufquam civilia campos."—

SIR,   June 17. 1796.

THOUGH the outlines of the French Revolution were completed in 1789, the more minute
parts of the work occupied a much longer time,
and were not underftood to be finally adjufted until the year 1791, when the Convention, invefted
with revolutionary powers, gave place to an ordinary legiflative affembly. During the period while
this great undertaking was in its progrefs, the
neighbouring potentates appear to have indulged
the malignant hope, that infuperable difficulties,
or fome finifter accidents, would prevent its completion ; but when, to their extreme difappointment
and mortification, they faw the whole fabric fuccefsfully and completely reared, there occurred
no other refource than to join, by main force, in
pulling it down.

For this purpofe, therefore, was concluded the
famous treaty of Pilnitz ; a treaty by which the
greater defpots of Europe, forgetting their former
feuds, and overlooking that oppofition of intereft
which had hitherto been continually exciting them
to overreach and undermine one another, united
in the common caufe of defpotifm, and became
bound, by themfelves, and with the affiftance of
all whom they could perfuade to embark in the

same enterprize, to overturn the new government in France, and to root out those obnoxious principles and opinions which had given rise to it.

From a publication which is believed to be authentic, it appears that the object of this treaty, was not only the invasion of France, and the restoration of its ancient government, but the partition of that country, and of Poland, among the principal contracting powers. The accomplishment of that object, in part, with respect to the Poles; the barbarous treatment which that people have experienced in the destruction, not only of their free constitution, but of their existence as an independent nation, leave no room to doubt what would have been the fate of the French, had their unprincipled and ambitious invaders been able to carry their designs into execution.

It seems impossible for any person, animated by the least spark of justice or humanity, to reflect, for a moment, without indignation and horror, upon a combination of this atrocious nature ; a combination against the liberties of mankind, by which a set of absolute princes, not contented with enslaving their own subjects, resolved to maintain by force a system of slavery in other countries ; arrogated the power of dictating a form of government to a foreign independent state ; and while they required that the people should renounce that constitution which they had voluntarily adopted, laid hold of the opportunity for enriching and aggrandizing themselves by the wreck of

thofe dominions which they propofed to difmember. Such were the avowed fentiments of thofe
combined powers; the bafis of their affociation
for the conqueft of France, in which the other
ftates of Europe were invited to concur, and to
contribute their affiltance. It was expected, it
feems, that the other European nations would join
in this confederacy; but how far this expectation
arofe from any particular affurances to this purpofe actually given, or from the general belief
that they would feel a common intereft in fup-
preffing the late political innovations in France,
the public has·not yet been fufficiently informed.

In purfuance of this treaty, the Duke of Brunfwick, in fummer 1792, invaded France with an
army of about 90,000 men; having circulated, at
the fame time, a manifefto, in which he threatened military execution to fuch of the inhabitants as
dared to defend themfelves, and promifed fafety
and protection to all who fhould open their gates
to his troops; adding, withal, a declaration, that
he had no intention to meddle with the internal
government of France.

This was accompanied by another elaborate manifefto, in which the Emperor and the King of
Pruffia undertake the arduous tafk of vindicating
thefe violent meafures, by declaiming againft the
French Revolution, and by maintaining, with
great gravity, that the French King was poffeffed
of a *fupreme, never-ceafing, and indivifible au-*

thority, of which he neither could be deprived, nor could voluntarily divest himself.

With respect to the proceedings of the French, which are here the subject of such keen invectives, it is to be observed, that the establishment of their new constitution was attended with less tumult, disorder, or licentiousness, than from the nature of things could have been expected. And among the other circumstances arising from that great political change, the little bloodshed, which it had hitherto occasioned, is most especially worthy of notice. Though the French populace had, in some few cases, discovered remarkable ferocity in taking vengeance upon some obnoxious individuals ; yet, upon the whole, the number of lives destroyed, in a nation comprehending five-and-twenty millions, and in so great a revolution as that of changing an inveterate despotism into a very limited monarchy, had been incredible small.

It also merits attention, that hitherto the resolution of establishing a pure democracy had never been taken. There had, indeed, been great differences of opinion upon that subject, in what was called the *Constituent Assembly* ; but the majority had determined in favour of a limited monarchy ; and the partizans of a republic had formerly expressed their acquiescence in that determination. The circumstances of France, however, with respect to the other powers of Europe, had unavoidably weakened and discouraged the friends of monar-

chy ; and had no lefs confirmed and ftrengthened
the adherents of republican government. During the impending quarrel with thofe powers, and
after the war was publicly declared, or diftinctly
forefeen, fufpicions that the king was difpofed to
fupport the enemies of France, and was engaged
in a fecret correfpondence with them, were almoft
unavoidable. In that critical fituation, the continuance of monarchical government became, perhaps, impracticable.

I do not enter into the queftion, how far the
fovereign had really formed a confpiracy with
thofe foreign powers, and with that part of his
own family engaged in the fame caufe, for the
purpofe of reftoring the government handed down
by his anceftors, which had been fo recently and
fo violently overturned. Suppofing him to have been
involved in that confpiracy, his fituation, if it could
not entirely juftify, will be admitted to palliate at
leaft, and, in fome meafure, to excufe his behaviour. The hardfhips and infults to which he
had been expofed, the total want of the confidence of his own fubjects which he experienced,
and the abfolute confinement to which he was fubjected ; not to mention the loud voice of his ancient nobility, deprived of their eftates, and ba-
nifhed from their native country ; the intrigues of
an artful and ambitious queen, whofe fpirit was
not broken by her misfortunes ; together with the
flattering promifes of fo many powerful fovereigns
who had warmly efpoufed his intereft, and had re-

folved to hazard every thing for the recovery of
his prerogative; thefe afforded, perhaps, temptations too powerful, and feducing, to be refifted by
a perfon of his feeble and flexible character. But
whatever was the real ftate of the fact, the fufpicions entertained againft him were too univerfal,
and had too much the air of probability to render
it prudent for the French Nation to commit their
rights and liberties to the cuftody of fo equivocal
a guardian.

The effects produced upon the minds of the
French people by the Duke of Brunfwick's invafion, and by fuch a powerful combination againft
them will be the fubject of another letter.

I am, &c.

Crito.

LETTER VI.

TO THE EDITOR OF THE SCOTS CHRONICLE.

SIR,   June 24. 1796.

It is impoffible to conceive a fituation
more deplorable and defperate than that into
which the French, from the circumftances mentioned in my former letter, were now reduced.
Invaded by a force which they could have no
hope of being able to refift, and profecuted with
a degree of animofity and rancour which would
be fatisfied with nothing lefs than utter extermi-
nation, they appeared to have no other alterna-

tive, than either to fubmit implicitly to their enemies, or to fell their lives and liberties at the
higheft price, and to die in the laft ditch. Without hefitation they chofe the latter; and, by the
impulfe of that determination, they were exalted
to a pitch of heroic enthufiafm, which rendered
them fuperior to all the nations of the earth.

The firft meafure that feemed indifpenfible in
this dreadful conjuncture, was to eftablifh a pure
democracy. Their king, according to their unanimous opinion, was not to be trufted. His flight
to Varennes, from which he was brought back by
force, and his difputes with the National Affembly, concerning the appointment of his minifters,
and concerning the interpofition of his negative
to the public decrees, had prepared the way to
an immediate rupture. The manifefto of the
Duke of Brunfwick appeared in Paris about the
7th of Auguft 1792. Alarm and terror feized
the inhabitants; and, on the 10th of that month,
produced a violent attack upon the king's palace,
with the deftruction of the Swifs guards. This
was followed by the bloody tragedy exhibited on
the 2d of September, which appears to have been
the effect of fudden rage and refentment excited
by the progrefs of the danger.

The friends of republican government, who
now gained the afcendant, were divided into two
factions. The Parifian populace, who, feeling the
influence which, from their numbers, and their vi-
cinity to the feat of government, they were likely

to maintain over the legillature, wished as much
as pollible to equalize the different ranks, to ex-
pel or extinguilh the fuperior clais of inhabitants,
and to annihilate every monument or veltige of
the ancient diltinctions. The people in the provinces, who poſleſſed no fuch influence, adopted a
milder fyitem of policy; and being jealous of the
authority likely to be attained by the capital, were
fufpected of intending to divide the monarchy into independent diltricts, and to connect them by a
federal union. The leaders of the latter party
were men of great liberality and benevolence, and
fome of them not without eloquence and talents;
but they feem to have been deltitute of that capacity, vigour, and boldneſs, which their perilous fituation demanded. The oppoſite party were directed by perſons of a different defcription; men
of a lower education, but of greater intrepidity,
and who feemed to fcruple at nothing, in order to
attain their purpoſes. At the head of theſe was
the noted Robefpierre, a man poſſeſſed of no brilliant accomplilhments, but of deep penetration,
and boundlefs ambition; awed by no principle;
reitrained by no feelings of humanity. This man
courted the populace with unwearied attention;
and he feems to have obtained their implicit confidence. He adopted all their peculiar interelts
and opinions. He feems to have been a real en-
thuſiaſt; and, however ltrongly actuated by the
l ve of power, was never fufpected of pecuniary
corruption. Though his character as a man has

been held in deferved execration, it may, perhaps,
be affirmed with truth, that he was the only perfon in the nation capable, in that critical period,
of defending his country from its numerous enemies. To gratify the Parifian mob, as well as to
eftablifh his own authority, he fhed without mercy
the blood of every perfon who oppofed his defigns. But fuch was the unhappy fituation of
France, that an abfolute fubmiffion to the executive
government was become indifpenfibly necefiary.
Had any oppofite party to that which was upper-
moft been fuffered to raife its head, it would immediately have been joined and fupported by the
foreign powers; and this would have produced
fuch internal commotion, as would have prevented
the extraordinary exertions which the prefervation
of the conftitution required.

It is not my intention to vindicate thefe violent
meafures, but to point out the perfons at whofe
door the principal guilt muft lie; and, however
we may blame the numerous violations of juftice
and humanity, exhibited in thofe fcenes of blood
and horror, we muft always remember that they
proceeded, in a great meafure, from the hoftile
powers who threatened France with inevitable deftruction. By them a great part of thofe cruelties
had been rendered unavoidable. The enemies of
the *firft revolution*, in that devoted country, were
in reality the authors of the *fecond*. Had the
French been left to fettle their own government
according to their own ideas of expediency, the

mild and inoffensive character of their sovereign
would, probably, never have rendered him the object of their distrust and resentment; and the form
of government, suggested and established by their
own free choice, would have remained with little
alteration or disturbance. Had they not been ter-
rified, and reduced to despair, by an invasion,
which no ordinary force could resist, conducted
by an unrelenting and sanguinary enemy, who did
not seem to look upon them as fellow creatures,
but as beasts of prey, to be hunted down, and ex-
terminated from the face of the globe, there is no
ground to believe that those tragical and shocking
events, so inconsistent with the character of a po-
lished nation, would ever have appeared. These
are truths which ought to be seriously considered
by those persons who declaim with so much noise
upon the barbarity of the late transactions in France,
and who exult with such indecent triumph, in the
reflection that the revolution in that country, in-
stead of being an object of imitation, is now beheld, by the rest of Europe, with disgust and
aversion.

The unfortunate issue of the Duke of Bruns-
wick's invasion must have tended to convince the
surrounding nations of two important facts : The
first, that the attachment of the French nation to
liberty, and their hatred to the old government,
were insuperable : The second, that the enthusiasm
with which that people were animated, was sufficient to counterbalance the advantages of military

fkill and difcipline, and had, in fact, rendered
their new levied militia fuperior to the molt regular armies which Europe could produce.

The world has been long dazzled by the *eclat*
of military glory, and led, it fl. uld feem, to ef-
timate military talents above their juft value. Mr.
Hume was thought to indulge in his ufual love of
paradox, when he wrote an effay to prove, that a
higher exertion of genius is requifite to form a
great poet than to form a great general, and that
Homer and Milton were greater men than Alex-
ander or Cæfar. This effay has been fuppreffed
in the latter editions of his works; but were that
acute author now alive, he would own that his
affertion falls greatly fhort of the truth. The late
military events in Europe have reduced the Tu-
rennes, the Marlboroughs, and the Ferdinands,
to mere ordinary men. Experience has fhown, in
how fhort a time an army may be equipt, both in
point of officers and men, and taught to conquer
the beft appointed and difciplined troops in the
world. But furely we cannot entertain very lofty
ideas of a profeffion, in which eminence may be
fo eafily and fo quickly attained. It feems to require intrepidity and cool judgment, but no extraordinary abilities.

The decifive battle of Jemappe, which followed the Duke of Brunfwick's retreat, afforded conviction to every man of common fenfe, not mifled
by prejudice, that all attempts to conquer France,

with a view of restoring the old monarchy, must
be idle and chimerical.   I am, &c.

CRITO.

LETTER VII.

TO THE EDITOR OF THE SCOTS CHRONICLE.

SIR,   July 1. 1796.

THE friends of liberty in Britain could not
behold the violent measures of the Europe an des-
pots without extreme concern and uneasiness. It afforded ground for the most melancholy reflections,
to consider, that despotism, in so many kingdoms,
was not only maintained by each interior government, but was further to be protected by a sort of
imperial authority assumed over all, imposing a
negative upon the establishment of liberty in each
particular state.   Henry the IV. of France is
said to have formed the plan of preventing wars,
by an appeal to the determination of a supreme
council, upheld by an union of different nations.
The present combination supposed a *great council*,
not of nations, but of sovereigns ; not in behalf of
the rights of mankind, but in support of tyranny
and oppression.

It would be superfluous to observe, that, by
persons of an opposite description, by the aristo-
cracy, by the retainers of prerogative, and by a
great part of the corporate bodies in the kingdom,
these transactions upon the continent were viewed
in a very different light.   The reformation of

abufes at home, the introduction of a more ade-
quate reprefentation in the Houfe of Commons,
began to ftare them in the face, as the neceffary
effect of the fuccefsful exertions in France.

The Britifh miniftry have folemnly difclaimed
any acceffion to the treaty of Pilnitz; and it is
impoffible to difbelieve their affertion in a matter
which, however the particulars may have hitherto
been concealed, muft at length be completely di-
vulged. The truth feems to be, they entertained
no doubt that the invafion of France, by the Duke
of Brunfwick, would gain the end propofed without their affiftance. But no fooner had that enterprize been found entirely abortive, than they
were thrown into the utmoft confternation, and
refolved to take a principal fhare in the confederacy. The fpeech-making talents of the prime
minifter, it feems, could fuggeft no better expedient for diffipating thofe clouds with which he began to be encompaffed.

In this refolution he was confirmed by a great
addition of ftrength, which he received from a
powerful defection among the leaders in oppofition.
It had for fome time been rumoured, that certain
diftinguifhed members of the whig-party had been
planet-ftruck by the progrefs of French opinions;
and they now were induced, in fpite of the detefta-
tion of the principles of miniftry which they had
always avowed, to join the minifterial phalanx,
and to accept of places under government.

Though the public is not very apt to judge fa-
vourably of men who come into office by leaving
their party, and is difpofed to pay little attention
to the pretences which happen, in fuch cafes, to
be affumed, it muft be confeffed, that thefe perfons
have, on this occafion, been treated with unufual
candour. They have been fuppofed to act from
general ariftocratic prejudices more than from
private views of intereft. Even their enemies
muft admit, when the proud ftation which they
abandoned is taken in connection with the humble
fituation which they now enjoy, that their conduct
has been dictated, neither by the love of fame,.
nor by the love of power. In reality they have
been pitied more than cenfured; and their underftandings have been made the *fcape-goat* of their
feelings. The fame indulgence, however, has not
been extended to the inferior agents, included in
this migration; who, at the fame time that they
willingly embraced the opportunity of ferving their
country, are underftood to have felt no reluctance
at quitting the cold and thanklefs climate of oppofition for the genial funfhine of court favour. Even
the fanciful admirer of the age of chivalry, who
appears to have formerly difplayed the gilded co-
lours of liberty as a mere light horfeman of arif-
tocracy, now forgetting *the fublime* and *the beautiful*, was glad to retire upon a moft extravagant
penfion; and had the effrontery to laugh at his
former profeflions, by ftating the price of his apof-
tacy as the reward of his fervices, and by fubmit-

ting to a miferable recantation, in the form of a humilitating panegyric upon the leaft brilliant, and formerly the leaft admired of all his prefent bene-factors.

To prepare the nation for feconding the defigns of miniftry, and to provide a force capable of pre-venting all refiftance, no common efforts were fuf-ficient. The defire of obtaining a reform in the national reprefentation had produced numerous meetings of the people, in the mercantile towns, and in other parts of the kingdom, for the purpofe of petitioning parliament in fupport of that fa-vourite object. Many publications appeared, at the fame time, in which the general principles of government, and various political doctrines, were handled with great freedom. In fome of thefe, it muft be confeffed, that the Britifh Conftitution was treated with little refpect. But whatever might be the wanton fpeculations, or the licentious or foolifh expreffions of a few individuals, there is no ground to believe, that any confiderable number were defirous of a Republican fyftem, or that the great body of the people were not warmly attach-ed to that form of limited monarchy under which they have lived, and of which the happy effects have been fo long experienced. Minifters, how-ever, affected to think very differently; and en-deavoured to propagate an opinion, that the lower claffes of the people, inftigated by French emiffa-ries, and feduced by French politics, had entered into a confpiracy for the total overthrow of our

government. Every engine was now employed
for exciting apprehenfions of difloyalty and fedi-
tion. Societies were fet on foot, to procure information, to circulate reports, to propagate political
doctrines favourable to the views of their employ-
ers, and to prepare materials for the profecution
and conviction of the fuppofed offenders. At the
head of thefe, one Reeves, a retainer of the law,
and poffeffing an office under government, was diftinguifhed by his indefatigable zeal and activity.
At a later period, after the nation had recovered,
in fome meafure, from the delufion which then
prevailed, the conduct of this perfon appeared in
fuch a light to the public, that the Houfe of Commons thought proper to order a profecution againft
him by the Attorney General.. This meafure, towards a perfon in his fubordinate capacity, marks.
fufficiently the indignation which was felt.   It is
neceffary to obferve, that, in the trial which followed, the fact was found to be proved ; but he
has been acquitted from favourable circumftances
with refpect to his intentions.

   The artificial cry, which was thus raifed by de-
figning politicians, communicated real alarm and
terror to the honeft undefigning part of the inhabitants. The gentry expected to be degraded
from their rank by the French fyftem of *equality*.
Thofe who had any thing to lofe regarded themfelves as the immediate prey of *republicans* and *levellers*. Men of peaceable difpofitions, who hated
innovation, and were attached to the Britifh Con-

ftitution, trembled with the apprehenfion of fome
terrible convulfion, and of feeing the anarchy and
the cruelties, which had prevailed in France, introduced into their own country. It was in vain
to reprefent, that no veftige of infurrection, confpiracy, or defign to overturn the government,
could be found in any part of the kingdom. The
continual ferment which agitated the public mind,
prevented a fair examination, and contributed to
diftort and exaggerate every object.

Having fucceeded in raifing a panic in the higher claffes of the community, the next aim of Miniftry, in conjunction with all thofe who had a private intereft in avoiding a reform of the National
Reprefentation, was to recommend a war with
France, from whofe uncommon exertions had proceeded all the dangers with which this ifland appeared to be threatened. Some of the arguments
employed for this purpofe, which are of a fingular
nature, I fhall take the liberty of mentioning on a
future occafion. I am, &c.

CRITO.

LETTER VIII.

TO THE EDITOR OF THE SCOTS CHRONICLE.

SIR, July 12. 1796.

THE Britifh Miniftry having refolved upon
a war with France, their next point, in the natural
order of things, was to. find arguments in fupport
of that meafure. A celebrated writer of the laft

age has faid, that it was eafier to find *monks* than *reafons*. Matters have, fince that time, been ftrangely altered. Monachifm has not been thriving; and the reafoning faculty has been greatly improved. Reafons for going to war with France have occurred in fufficient abundance to furnifh a new fyftem of logic; as the eloquence difplayed upon the occafion might fupply an equally new fyftem of rhetoric. With refpect to the *morality* to be gathered from either of thefe, it feems, to fpeak in the mildeft terms, a little *cafuiftical*.

One of the chief reafons which has been advanced for going to war with France is, that this meafure appears abfolutely neceffary for checking, in this country, the progrefs of *French opinions*. This is the celebrated argument which logicians call the *argumentum baculinum*. If you do not give up your opinion, I will break your head. It has been pufhed, however, in this cafe, a little further than is commonly done. I will not only break the head of you, who entertain the offenfive opinion; but I will break the head of that fcoundrel who has perfuaded you to embrace it.

By French opinions, in the language of the knowing ones, are underftood fentiments favourable to a reform of Parliamentary Reprefentation; but, as reprefented to fincere, undefigning alarmifts, are meant defigns to overturn our monarchy, and to eftablifh a democratical government, with a complete equalization of rank and property, added to all the evils of anarchy, and a civil war, for God knows how long.

That there is any Englishman, or at least any confiderable number of Englishmen, who can entertain French opinions, in this latter fenfe, appears to be advanced without any proof, and without the leaft fhadow of probability. If there be any one political principle more prevalent than another in the inhabitants of this ifland, it is a fond prepoffeffion in favour of our own Conftitution, and an attachment to the Houfe of Hanover, in whom the crown was eftablifhed by the authority of parliament, and by whofe acceffion we were fecured from the tyranny of the lineal heir.

But fuppofing, for the fake of argument, that a number of perfons in Britain were fo wrong-headed as to entertain fuch opinions, would it follow, that going to war, either with them, or with France upon their account, is a proper expedient for guarding againft the confequences of fuch a pernicious way of thinking? Is force the beft inftrument for preventing poifonous doctrines, either religious or political? Has not the contrary been found by the experience of all ages? Was not the perfecution of Chriftianity, by the Roman government, the great natural means which contributed to fpread that religion over the empire? Was not perfecution one of the great circumftances which promoted the Reformation? This tendency of the application of force, in matters of opinion, is what might be expected from the conftitution of human nature.

D

There is a pride in the heart of man which makes him refuse to be browbeaten, and renders him tenacious of those opinions which he is commanded to renounce. His indignation and resentment are kindled against the injustice of pretending to assume a dominion over his conscience. The sufferings, besides, to which he is exposed for persisting in what he thinks the cause of truth, never fail to excite compassion; at the same time that the resolution and courage which he is prompted to display, raise admiration and esteem; sentiments which interest us for the sufferer, and create a strong prepossession in favour of his opinions.

There may, doubtless, be a persecution so powerful and sanguinary as to overcome these obstacles, and to extirpate the offensive tenets against which it is pointed; but this would require such a degree of tyranny, barbarity, and cruelty, and is so inconsistent with the manners of an enlightened and civilized age, that in the present state of most of the European nations, it may be supposed utterly impracticable; and every persecution, which is not effectual in exterminating opinions, must, of course, tend to aggravate and to promote them. If you mean to recommend a book to the public notice and approbation, you cannot practise a more successful method than by causing it to be burnt by the hangman. By making war upon French opinions, you have thus bestowed upon them an importance and consideration which they could not otherwise have attained. Your imprudence, not to

fay your injuſtice, has in ſome meaſure gilded and
varniſhed them over, and given them a degree of
currency, to which, of themſelves, they had no
title. After all, why may not the inhabitants of this
iſland enjoy the right of private judgment in ſpe-
culating upon their government? Is our Conſtitution ſo crazy and rotten, that it will not bear the.
handling? Is our limited monarchy, of which we
have ſo long boaſted, and which has been purchaſ-
ed by the blood of our forefathers, ſo little conſo-
nant to the principles of true liberty; ſo ill adapted
to the ſtate of the community, that we dare not
bring it to the teſt of reaſon? Is it ſo ill contrived,
that it requires a myſterious veil to cover its defects? or if otherwiſe, will not reaſon and truth ſe-
cure a great majority of the nation in oppoſition
to folly and error? Why truly, if our political
ſyſtem is not ſuch as will recommend itſelf to the
nation at large; if, upon a full and fair examination,
it does not appear ſuited to the great ends of government, I am afraid it muſt fall; and all our attempts to preſerve it by myſtery and concealment
will be to no purpoſe. But why, in the name of
wonder, ſhould this diſmal and groundleſs appre-
henſion be countenanced by the Britiſh Miniſters?

The alarming progreſs of the French arms, after the retreat of the Duke of Brunſwick, afforded another reaſon for going to war with that formidable nation. By their enthuſiaſtic ardour, and
by their amazing exertions, they were become a

match for all Europe; they had over-run the
Auſtrian Netherlands, ſo as to threaten the immediate invaſion of Holland ; and they had iſſued a
decree, offering fraternization to all thoſe nations who might be deſirous of eſtabliſhing a free
government. Neceſſity therefore, it was ſaid, obliged us to take arms in our own defence, and to
provide for our own ſafety before it was too late.
The balance of power has ever been accounted a
great political object among the potentates of modern Europe ; and to maintain this balance has always been held a ſufficient cauſe for entering into
a war. In the preſent caſe, the French were likely not only to deſtroy the external boundaries of
dominion, but even to ſweep away the ſyſtems of
government which had formerly ſubſiſted.

It was a little unlucky, that thoſe who ſtated
this argument, at the ſame time that they beheld
with ſuch terror theſe military operations, were
obliged to ſhut their eyes upon the no leſs alarming tranſactions in Poland. In violation of all
treaties, and in contempt of every law divine and
human, that miſerable country was torn to pieces,
and divided among. thoſe very princes with whom
Britain had combined for maintaining a balance of
power ; and while the Britiſh miniſtry were endeavouring to rouſe all Europe for oppoſing the
arms of the French nation, they were acquieſceing,
without a murmur, in the dreadful devaſtation, and
in the violent political convulſion, which their
own allies had produced in another quarter.

With regard to the danger apprehended from
the conqueft of other countries by France, there
are two confiderations, which hardly any perfon of
plain fenfe, and of ordinary information, can poffibly overlook. In the firft place, by whom were
the French driven to the neceffity of becoming an
armed nation, and of invading the neighbouring
ftates ? Before the treaty of Pilnitz, they had expreffed ftrong refolution againft foreign wars, and
feemed to have no defire of extending their own
dominions. They had indeed invaded Avignon,
and the bifhopric of Bafle, together with certain
territories in Lorrain, and Alface, belonging to
particular princes or ftates of the empire. As
thofe territories were locally fituated within the
kingdom of France, it had been judged effentially
requifite, for the fafety of the new eftablifhment,
that they fhould be annexed to the French monarchy ; while a pecuniary compenfation was allowed to the proprietors. Not to mention any
difputes concerning the *title* of the perfons who
had held thofe poffeffions, this tranfaction proceeded upon a principle of general utility, fimilar to
that which has been underftood to juftify our government in obliging the Duke of Athol to fell
the fovereignty of the Ifle of Man, or in obliging
the feudal lords in Scotland to refign, to the
crown, their heritable jurifdictions. But the foreign ftates, who afterwards invaded France, and
whofe territories were now over-run by the French,
had drawn that misfortune upon themfelves by

their unprovoked aggreffion. The French had
acted, in this cafe, upon a principle of retaliation,
which no impartial obferver, who is acquainted
with the law of nations, will venture to condemn.
As to their offering fraternity and affiftance to
other ftates defirous of eftablifhing a free government, it feems to have been a mere bravado, intended to counteract the effects of the general
combination of defpots, by which all the other
powers of Europe, and even the French people
themfelves, were invited to join in reftoring the
old government of France. But whatever was intended by this general declaration, as they never
had acted upon it, I cannot help thinking it was
incumbent upon us to require an explanation of
their intentions, before we made it the ground of
a war which was likely to be attended with very
ferious confequences.

The other confideration, to which I alluded, refpects the meafures which Britain ought to have
purfued on that occafion, for preventing the effu-
fion of blood, and reftoring peace to Europe.
Had Britain, at that period, offered her mediation
between the contending powers, is there any perfon who believes that the French would not have
gladly accepted the offer, and have been willing
to conclude a peace with their enemies, upon condition that each party fhould refign its foreign ac-
quifitions? But we feem to have thought that
France, after being pillaged by Pruffia and the
Emperor, and after having retaliated thofe hofti-

lities, fhould immediately relinquifh her conqueft,
fo as to give her enemies time to breathe, and prepare for a new invafion. Was it not the duty of
our miniftry, as the guardians of our lives and our
property, to fet on foot, in that critical conjuncture,
a negotiation for the purpofe which I have mentioned ? They not only neglected to do fo, but they
pofitively refufed to negociate, and to receive ex-
planations, though repeatedly, and with apparent
anxiety, offered them by the French. Does not
this abundantly fhow, that the danger of conqueft
by the French was a mere bugbear, fet up by thofe
perfons to terrify and delude the nation ; and that,
fo far from wifhing to force a peace, as they might
eafily have done, by offering to guarantee a reafonable treaty, and by threatening, upon the refufal of either party, to throw the weight of Britain
into the oppofite fcale, our minifters were in reality
defirous of joining the framers of the league of
Pilnitz, and of entering into a war of extermina-
tion againft France, not for the reafons which they
affigned, but from other motives beft known to
themfelves ? I am, &c.

CRITO.

LETTER IX.

SIR,   July 19. 1796.

THE cruelties committed by the French,
together with the danger apprehended to the lives

of the king and the royal family, were alfo ftrongly urged as a reafon for going to war with that
barbarous people. This became a topic of declamation, upon which the unfledged orator was happy to try his wings, and the crafty politician found
an opportunity of difplaying, at an eafy rate, both
his humanity and his loyalty.

Every perfon poffeffed of common feeling muft
be fhocked with a recital of thofe barbarities; and
human nature revolts againft any attempt to excufe
or to palliate them. We cannot, however, fufficiently exprefs our aftonifhment at the effrontery
with which the ultimate authors of thefe enormi-
ties, the framers of the treaty of Pilnitz, who, by
their invafion of France, had driven the people to
thefe defperate meafures, were ftudioufly kept out
of view and concealed. I am very far from thinking that every murder, or act of cruelty, committed by the French, was abfolutely neceffary, or
even expedient for extricating them from their difficulties. But a general courfe of extreme feverity was rendered unavoidable; and in fuch a cafe
it is not furprifing that the adminiftrators, thrown
into confternation by the magnitude of the danger,
fhould fometimes act from precipitate rafhnefs, and
fometimes lay hold of the occafion to gratify their
own paffions, or to court popularity by fuch rigor-
ous punifhments as were agreeable to the lower
clafs of citizens. The foreign potentates, therefore, who enabled thofe leaders to acquire and to
exercife fuch extraordinary powers, and who put

them into a fituation where fuch abufes were naturally to be expected, are certainly anfwerable
for that guilt which was incurred.

Though this confideration will not always juftify the immediate agents, it muft, in every cafe,
throw the principal blame upon thofe who could
not mifs to forefee the confequences, and yet perfifted in that line of conduct which infallibly produced them.

But whatever may be thought of the fpeculative humanity and loyalty of the inhabitants of
this country, in declaiming againft the cruelty and
injuftice committed by their neighbours, it does
not appear that thofe who recommended a war
with France, upon that account, were actuated by
a real principle of benevolence, or by a regard for
the life of Louis the XVIth ; fince nothing could
be more evidently calculated to augment and to
extend the cruelties complained of, and the mifchiefs that were apprehended. By joining the
league for compelling the French to reftore the
old government, the Britifh Minifters could not
fail to increafe the defpair, and defire of vengeance, which had produced fuch revolutionary
powers in the leaders of the multitude, and which
furnifhed a reafon for the murder of thofe who
had incurred any fufpicion of affifting the enemy.
Had Britain, on the contrary, declared againft a
war, and offered her mediation between the contending parties, thofe evils might have been greatly abated ; and the lives of the king and the royal

family might, in all probability, have been pro-
ferved. It is well known, that a numerous party
in the Convention wifhed to fave the life of the
King; and it can hardly be doubted that a great
majority would have concurred in this objeft, if
they could have purchafed by it the interpofition.
of Britain for ftopping the progrefs of their enemies. Why did our humane and loyal orators
neglect to fuggeft fuch an obvious. and falutary
meafure ? I am unwilling to credit, what has been
infinuated with fome colour of probability, that
many, who cenfured with fo much acrimony the
conduct of the French, were fecretly pleafed with
fuch barbarity and cruelty, as being calculated to
throw an odium upon the Revolution, and to prevent, what was dreaded as the effect of it in this
country, the reform of parliamentary reprefentation. In this view, I cannot help recollecting an
obfervation, faid to have been imprudently hazard--
ed by a perfon of fome note, that the wretched
Marat was *the hen who laid golden eggs.*

The prefervation of the Chriftian religion was
another motive, by which thofe who had refolved
upon a war with France endeavoured to roufe the
nation, and to procure its unanimous exertions in
feconding that meafure.

It is a circumftance not the leaft remarkable in
the hiftory of the great political events of the
prefent age, that the late important revolutions in
America, and in France, unlike thofe in preced-
ing periods, have not been dictated, or promoted,

by any religious enthufiafm. It may even be obferved, that in France, men of letters, from the
wantonnefs of fpeculation, or from the affectation
of contradicting received opinions, have of late
frequently admitted a vein of irreligion and fcep-
ticifm into their writings. We are not, however,
to conclude from hence that the people in general
are tainted with principles of infidelity ; nor even,
perhaps, that thofe very writers have ferioufly
formed any practical fyftem hoftile to religion.
The firft revolution in France, by attempting a
radical reform in the prodigious inequality of
church livings, had provoked, as we may eafily
fuppofe, the indignation and refentment of the
higher orders of churchmen ; and multitudes of
the clergy, who thought it incumbent upon them
to refign their functions, rather than fubmit to a
degradation which they hoped would not be permanent, communicated, in the countries to which
they fled, an alarm that the French, among other
changes, intended nothing lefs than the total overthrow of the Chriftian religion. Even the clergy
who had been content to remain in their own
country, were led to propagate fimilar reprefenta-
tions ; and thus a ftated oppofition and animofity
was created between them and the leaders of the
revolution ; while the former employed their whole
remaining power and influence in fupport of the
old government, and the latter, irritated by re-
peated provocations, became more and more dif-

pofed to limit or deſtroy that authority which the
church had formerly enjoyed.

It was, perhaps, with a view of diminiſhing the
influence of churchmen, though partly, too, from
an oſtentation of ſingularity, more than from thoſe
confiderations of utility which were avowed, that
that the French Convention afterwards introduced
a new calendar, dividing every month into *decades*,
inſtead of the former diviſion into weeks of ſeven
days, and in this manner pointing out one day in
ten, inſtead of the one day in ſeven, which by the
practice of early Chriſtians had been ſet apart for
the public obſervances of religion.

The impropriety and folly of this new regulation is obvious enough. For though the difference
between one day and another, in a matter of mere
external obſervance, is in itſelf not very material;
and though there be no particular precept of the
Goſpel recommending the firſt day of the week
for the peculiar purpoſe of public worſhip, yet the
alteration of a practice, in every reſpect ſo uſeful,
and confirmed by the uſage of many centuries, was
totally inconſiſtent with prudence, and might prove
a ſtumbling-block to many well difpoſed Chriſtians.

It would be great weakneſs, however, to believe, that the Chriſtian religion in general, or
even in France, can be materially injured, either
by this regulation, or by the petulant and abſurd
oppoſition and deriſion which the vanity, or the
malice, of ſome individuals appears to have ſug-
geſted. Chriſtianity is founded upon a rock; and

neither Thomas Paine with his *Age of Reason*,
nor Anarchafis Cloots, with his *Reprefentative of
all Religions*, nor Fabre D'Eglantine, the abolifher
of Sunday, with his *New Calendar*, nor even that
profound philofopher who ftood up in the French
Affembly, and profeffed himfelf *an Atheift*, fhall
ever, as we are affured, from the beft authority,
prevail againft our holy religion. Chriftianity is
an enlightened fyftem, which introduced a purer
morality than had formerly prevailed in the world,
and more diftinct views of a future ftate of rewards
and punifhments, by which the efforts of human
laws for the fuppreffion of crimes are better en-
forced and promoted. The more the light of
truth is fpread over the world, the more clearly
are mankind enabled to fee their true intereft ;
and the more will they be convinced of the utility of fupporting a religion by which all the bands
of human fociety are thus maintained and ftrengthened.

But though the genuine principles of Chriftianity are in no danger, the adventitious trappings in
which it has been decked, for the purpofe of daz-
zling the multitude, are likely to be ftripped off,
and thrown away as mere ufelefs rags; myfterious
tenets, the invention of prieftcraft in the dark
ages, by which that religion was fo unworthily
debafed, and rendered the inftrument of undue influence and corruption, are likely to be exploded;
and the unbounded authority and dominion which
an ambitious and interefted clergy have fo long

E

exercifed over the rights of private judgment and
of confcience, are likely to crumble down, and
to be trodden under foot. The Roman Catholic
fuperftition, that gigantic monfter which has drunk
fo much human blood, that dragon which has long
guarded the den of ignorance, and held more than
the half of Europe in the chains of moral and political flavery, feems now to be faft approaching
his laft agonies.

With regard to the religious opinions entertained in France, it cannot efcape obfervation, that
how difagreeable foever they may be to us, it is
the height of imprudence and abfurdity to make
war upon our neighbours for the purpofe of producing a reformation in this particular. The
world has too long experienced the effects of religious perfecutions and wars, not to have learned
the falutary leffon, that mankind, thofe efpecially
who belong to different nations, fhould bear with
one another in their differences of religious opinion. It feems evident, at the fame time, that the
fyftem of policy to which the French government
is now rapidly advancing, is that of allowing an
unbounded liberty of confcience; of protecting
all different fects, provided they are not enemies
to the civil conftitution; and of leaving to the
members of every fect the privilege of choofing,
and the tafk of maintaining their own religious
teachers. This, every one knows, is conformable
to the principles of the *independents* in England,
a fect, whofe uniform zeal in the caufe of pure and

genuine Chriftianity is unqueftionable; and it
feems to be the fyftem of religious policy which
is now realifed in the North American States.
For my own part, though I feel, from education,
an attachment to the forms of religion eftablifhed
in this country, and am fenfible that innovation,
in matters of this kind, ought never to be attempted without very cogent reafons; yet, were I the
inhabitant of a country, where, from good grounds,
the old eftablifhment had been abolifhed, I fhould,
without hefitation, prefer this very liberal and apparently beneficial fyftem.

It is eafy to fee, however, that the averfion dif-
covered by the leading people in France to religious eftablifhments, has tended to excite a jealoufy in the eftablifhed clergy of other countries,
and to produce a fet of *religious alarmifts*, willing
to reprefent the whole nation as hoftile to Chriftianity, and even to all religion. In fuch a fituation, it is not furprifing, that many individuals of
our eftablifhed church, whether in confequence of
their own apprehenfions, or in the capacity of fti-
pendiaries to the executive government, fhould be
ready, upon this point, to diftinguifh themfelves
in the fervice of adminiftration. Even in Scotland,
where the very moderate provifion of the clergy
allows very fcanty rewards to extraordinary merit,
many laudable attempts have not been wanting to
roufe the people on account of the dangers to religion arifing from the French Revolution. It
fhould feem, however, that the populace in this

E ij

country, though certainly not fufpe&ed of luke-
warmnefs in matters of religion, yet, whether from
an acquaintance with the real ftate of the facts, or
from a want of confidence in the intentions of thofe
political paftors, or from whatever caufes, have
hitherto paid very little attention. to fuch publications. I am, &c.

CRITO.

LETTER X.

TO THE EDITOR OF THE SCOTS CHRONICLE.

SIR,   Auguft 2. 1796.

THE chief reafons which were given for in-
volving us in a French war have now been confidered ; and I cannot help thinking, that, though
they have been turned and twifted into a great
variety of fhapes, and prefented in different lights,
with all the addrefs which human ingenuity could
employ, their futility and abfurdity muft, at the
firft glance, be apparent. They were fit only to
make an impreffion upon imaginations already dif-
ordered by fear, and warped by prejudice. There
were two other topics employed on this occafion,
of which a very flight notice will be fufficient ;
becaufe, though they were much infifted upon,
both in public and in private difcourfe, and had
probably fome weight at the time, they feem now
to be univerfally and completely difregarded.

The firft was the decree of the French Convention for opening the. navigation of the Scheldt

from Antwerp, intended to promote the trade of
the Belgic provinces, now in the poffeffion of
France. This meafure is capable of being viewed
in different lights; as, on the one hand, it put an
end to a monopoly which, like all reftrictions of
that nature, was, doubtlefs, hurtful to the general
intereft of commerce; and, on the other, it was
held prejudicial to the peculiar trade of the Dutch,
to whom, by fome old treaties, that monopoly had
been fecured. Which of thefe confiderations is of
the greateft importance I fhall not pretend to determine; but certain it is, that the Britifh miniftry, in 1786, had concurred in the views of the
Emperor, who then, for the benefit of the Netherlands, had thoughts of eftablifhing the free
navigation of that river. A Britifh Ambaffador
was then fent to Antwerp, for the purpofe of exciting the inhabitants to beftir themfelves in foli-
citing the Emperor for the attainment of this commercial object; fo different were the political
views entertained by the fame perfons within fo
fhort a period. That nations, that is, miniflers,
as well as private individuals, fhould change their
opinions, and their fyftems of conduct, according
to their different political combinations, is agreeable to common experience; but that fo frivolous
a matter, an injury fo entirely diplomatic, fhould
be regarded as a folid ground for rufhing immediately into a dangerous and expenfive war, is truly
furprifing. It might be a proper fubject of re-
monftrance or complaint, but could never afford,

to perfons, not vifited with infanity, an inducement
for plunging a great nation into an abyfs of blood
and mifery, without attempting, by a previous negociation, to avert that calamity. The States of
Holland themfelves, it is well known, the parties
underftood to be immediately injured, but who
had not our private reafons, were much lefs cap-
tious ; and it was with the utmoft difficulty that,
by the authority of the Stadtholder, under the
influence of the Britifh Court, they could be prevailed upon to fecond our defigns.

In mentioning the ftate of the Dutch, upon
whofe account we profeffed that we were led immediately into the war, it feems impoffible to a-
void remarking, that our behaviour to that people,
from firft to laft, appears not a little extraordinary ; and nothing, it fhould feem, but the ancient
commercial jealoufy, through which we are apt to
view their circumftances, could prevent us from
reflecting upon it with fhame and regret. Having
dragged them into the war, we no fooner found
it inconvenient to perfift in the defence of their
country, than we left them to fhift for themfelves ; not for the purpofe of making peace, for
that might have been excufable, but with a view
to carry on the war in a different manner, by fub-
fidizing Pruffia and the Emperor. When the
Dutch were, of confequence, reduced under the
power of their enemies, and did what, in thofe
hard circumftances, imperious neceffity compelled
them to do, we immediately feized their property,

subjected them to every species of hostility, and have at this day scarce any other acquisitions to boast of but those which we have obtained from the plunder of these our ancient allies. In what manner we can vindicate our conduct to that long-suffering people, it were to be wished that our minister, when he can spare so much time under the pressure of his present financial difficulties, would have the goodness to explain.

The other topic which I proposed to mention is one, to which, in private conversation, men have usually resorted after trying, unsuccessfully, to vindicate the war upon every other ground. The French, it is said, were the first to make war upon us. We had no choice, but were reduced to the fatal necessity of defending ourselves. Those ambitious republicans had formed the design of extending their dominion, and of planting their tree of liberty over the whole of Europe, if not over the whole globe. In pursuance of this object they made war upon us, whenever it suited their purpose ; and we had no alternative left, but that of implicit submission, or of providing for our own safety by a timely resistance. Whether any person ever believed this assertion, I very much doubt. It is at least pretty clear that nobody believes it at present.

For enabling us to judge of this point, a very slight review of the circumstances of the case will be sufficient. That the first verbal declaration of war proceeded from the French Convention, on

the 1st of February 1793, is indisputable. But
the conduct of the British Court, long before that
period, had been such as clearly to evince its hostile intentions, and in reality amounted to an une-
quivocal declaration of hostilities. Soon after the
10th of August 1792, the British Ambassador to
the French Court was recalled. Upon the meeting of Parliament about the end of that year, the
debates were carried on in a strain of arrogant
invective and declamation against the French,
which abundantly showed a resolution to keep no
measures with that people. The proposal of negociation, which had been urged by Opposition,
was again and again rejected with disdain, as dif-
graceful to the British Crown; and Mr. Burke
repeatedly declared, without the least contradic-
tion, or mark of disapprobation from his ministerial
friends, that *the two states might already be considered as actually engaged in war:* From an idea
of starving the inhabitants, our ministry, in the
mean time, laid an embargo upon the exportation
of corn to that country, though the market was
then open to other nations. The Alien Bill, soon
after, was introduced into parliament, which being
considered as an infraction of the commercial
treaty with France, M. Chauvelin, the French
Ambassador, in very respectful terms, remonstrated
against it; but so far from meeting with any attention from our ministers, he was peremptorily
ordered to quit the kingdom within eight days,

and the order was inserted by authority in the London Gazette.

It is here worthy of remark, that by the commercial treaty above referred to, concluded in 1786, it was exprefsly declared, that, in cafe any fubject of mifunderftanding fhould arife between the two nations, *the fending away the Ambaffdor of one of them fhould be deemed a rupture.*

It is further to be obferved, that in regard to the two meafures of France which had given offence to the Britifh Court, the decree for the opening of the Scheldt, and that which offered fraternity to other nations, M. Chauvelin had, in explanation of thefe meafures, delivered an official note to the Secretary of State, on the 27th of December; and, upon the refufal of the Miniftry to treat with them, his explanation was confirmed by an immediate communication, in another note from the *French Executive Council.* In this note they declare, " that the decree of *fraternization* could " not be applicable, but to the fingle cafe, when " the general will of a nation, clearly and unequi- " vocally expreffed, fhould call for the affiftance " and fraternity of the French nation;" and, with refpect to their interference in the navigation of the Scheldt, they declare, as " the French na- " tion has renounced all conqueft, and only occu- " pies the Netherlands during the war; that as " foon as the Belgic nation fhall find itfelf in full " poffeffion of its liberty, and when its general " will may be declared legally and unfettered,

" then, if England and Holland shall affix any im-
" portance to the opening of the Scheldt, the Exe-
" cutive Council will leave that affair to a direct
" negociation with the Belgians themselves."

From an anxiety, as it should seem, to avoid a
rupture with England, the French Ministry, per-
ceiving the reluctance of the British Court to treat
with M. Chauvelin, dispatched M. Maret, under
Secretary for Foreign Affairs, to enter into a negociation with our Ministers. It has been asserted,
that M. Maret was instructed to offer to our Ministers; first, that the claim for opening the Scheldt
should be given up; secondly, that the French
troops should not advance beyond a certain dis-
tance from the Dutch territories; and, thirdly,
that the offensive decree of fraternization should
be repealed. The proposal of negociation with
M. Maret, however, was rejected by our Ministry in the same haughty and contemptuous manner as that with M. Chauvelin; notwithstanding
which, that Commissioner was sent from France a
second time, with enlarged powers, and with in-
structions, it is said, to offer still greater conces-
sions, with respect to their possessions in the West
Indies. His second mission, however, was equally
unsuccessful with the first; and he was ordered
immediately to depart from the kingdom.

Considering all these different circumstances, it
was certainly with a bad grace that our Ministry
pretended to be taken unawares, and to be driven
from a system of neutrality, by the declaration of.

war upon the part of France. Candour muſt o-
blige us to confeſs, that our behaviour was in the
higheſt degree offenſive and provoking; and that
it marked a determined purpoſe of proceeding to
immediate hoſtilities; while, on the contrary, the
conduct of the French teſtified an eager deſire to
avoid any rupture with Britain. In ſuch a caſe,
the verbal declaration of war by the French was
a mere matter of ceremony; though perhaps it
would have been more politic in them to have,
for ſome time longer, avoided this meaſure.

I am, &c.

CRITO.

LETTER XI.

TO THE EDITOR OF THE SCOTS CHRONICLE.

SIR, Auguſt 9. 1796.

After giving ſuch reaſons as were judged
expedient for entering into the war, it was further
neceſſary to inform the public of the preciſe object
for which it was undertaken. The former was
requiſite, that we might receive ſome ſatisfaction
concerning the propriety of the meaſure; the latter, that we might have an idea of the magnitude
and duration of the enterpriſe, and of the hazard
or expence which it might occaſion. It may eaſily
be imagined, that the explanation of this latter
point was a matter of ſome delicacy. There are
many caſes where the naked truth ought not raſhly
to be expoſed to the view of every by-ſtander.

To avow all at once the real object of the war,
confidering the circumftances formerly mentioned,
was inconfiftent with that referve and caution
which the nature of the cafe appeared to demand,
and might have prevented that future variation of
purpofe which the uncertain courfe of events might
poffibly fuggeft. Were it not for the ferious confequences which have been produced, and which
are ftill likely to follow, the various juggling tricks
that have been practifed, the different views which
have been held up at different periods, and the
fudden fhifting of the ground upon the feveral un-
expected turns of fortune, would be highly ludi-
crous. They prefent a chequered fcene of diffimulation and embarraffment, a fort of tragic diftrefs interwoven with a degree of comic dexterity,
fomething refembling the clergyman, in the farce,
who preaches againft popery, at the fame time
that he is picking your pocket; which, though not
perfectly confiftent with the unities of Ariftotle,
can hardly fail to exercife the rifible mufcles of
the moft phlegmatic fpectator.

The real and ultimate object of the war, as was
formerly obferved, has been invariably the preventing of a reform in our parliamentary reprefentation; and this, it was thought, required a
counter-revolution in France, by pulling down the
new conftitution, and reftoring the ancient defpotifm; meafures which could not be effected
without an entire conqueft of the country. But
this purpofe, which would, at the firft propofal,

have ftartled, perhaps, the moft determined adherent of prerogative, and have funk in defpair the
panic-ftruck alarmift, was carefully concealed.
The Jefuitical pretences which were affumed, at
the beginning, will for a long time be remember-
ed. To prepare the minds of people for engaging
in the conteft, and to preclude the fcruples which,
in the firft moments of deliberation, were likely
to occur, pofitive affurances were given that our
government had no intention to join in the objects
of thofe foreign potentates who had entered into
the treaty of Pilnitz. The war in which we were
about to engage was merely a defenfive war, and
had no other aim than to fecure ourfelves, and our
allies from the aggreffion of the French. After
the nation had once actually engaged in the war,
the national paffions, in the progrefs of the conteft, were likely to be inflamed ; and, in the eager-
nefs of victory, fcruples, which appeared at firft
infurmountable, would probably vanifh. Having
paffed the Rubicon, our retreat was, by every
new ftep, rendered more difficult, and our path
more intricate and perplexed. The minifter then
ventured to open his mind more fully, and to acknowledge that his object in the war included, not
only an indemnification for our expences, but the
eftablifhment of fuch a government in France as
could afford to Great Britain a fufficient fecurity
for the maintenance of her future tranquillity.

Such were the progreffive views held out, in
particular by Mr. Pitt, in his fpeech on the open-

ing of the budget in 1793, and in that upon the
motion for an addrefs to his Majefty, in January
1794. It was not difficult to fee, that upon the
fuppofition of the continuance of the war till our
miniftry were fatisfied with the fecurity afforded
by the government in France, the interpretation
of this article being referved to themfelves, a peace
might be deferred as long as they fhould find con-
venient. But, if any doubt had remained upon
that fubject, it was afterwards, in the debate concerning the employment of the French Emigrants
in our military fervice, removed by a pofitive declaration. The alarmifts having then arrived at
that pitch of enthufiafm to be ripe for the direct
avowal, it was at length plainly admitted by a
minifter, from the northern part of the ifland ; a
minifter who, in cafe it fhould prove difagreeable,
had not much popularity to lofe ; that the war
muft be continued, until we fhall be in a condition
to re-inftate the Emigrants in their former poffeffions ; that is, until we have not only overturned
the prefent order of things, but have by force of
arms, reftored the ancient defpotifm. The frank-
nefs of this avowal deferves commendation ; and,
if I miftake not, it was accompanied with fome
kind of apology, from confiderations of policy, for
not having been made at the beginning.

But that, from the beginning, the conqueft of
France, and the reftoration of the ancient defpotifm were intended, is manifeft from a variety of
circumftances. Not long after the commence-

ment of the war, I think in the beginning of April
1793, a propofal was made to Lord Grenville by
Le Brun the French minifter, for the re-eftablifhment of peace by an amicable negociation; and
to this end a paffport was demanded for an envoy
upon the part of France. But though the letters,
containing this application, fufficiently authenti-
cated, were laid before the Honourable Secretary
of State, they were totally difregarded, and, it
fhould appear, as much as poffible buried in fi-
lence. So favourable an opportunity of attempting at leaft to terminate the war, with honour to
the nation and crown, would not have been overlooked, unlefs a fixed refolution had been formed
of profecuting the conteft to the laft extremity.

The fuccefs of our arms towards the beginning
of the firft campaign, when, by the treachery of
Dumourier, the French were driven from Holland, and from the Auftrian Netherlands, and
their armies were almoft completely diforganifed,
prefented another opportunity, no lefs favourable,
for putting an end to the war; an opportunity
which, had our views terminated upon any thing
fhort of the entire conqueft of France, we fhould
certainly have been eager to feize. We had then
recovered all the poffeffions of our allies; and we
had reduced our enemy to fuch diftrefs as appeared to lay the foundation for an advantageous treaty. But though negociation was continually rung
in the ears of our miniftry, by the party in oppo-

F ij

i

fition at home, it was uniformly rejected with indignation.

The tone and language, indeed, of the combined powers varied a good deal, according to the
exigency of their affairs. They had no objection,
occafionally, to the employment of ftratagem for
promoting their ends; and it fhould feem that
they even fuffered, inadvertently, fuch terms of
accommodation to be offered, in their name, as
they had no ferious intention to fulfil. Upon the
agreement between the Prince of Saxe-Cobourg
and Dumourier, the latter publifhed a manifefto,
declaring, that his fole purpofe, in marching with
his army to Paris, was *to reflore the conflitution*
1789; and the Prince of Cobourg, in another
manifefto, relative to the foregoing, declares,
" that he will fupport, by all the force which is
entrufled to him, the generous and beneficent intentions of General Dumourier and his brave army." But the enterprife of Dumourier having totally failed of fuccefs, there was held at Antwerp, on the 8th of April, that is, three days after the above declaration was publifhed, a con-
grefs of the reprefentatives of the combined powers, at which the Duke of York and Lord Auck-
land were prefent on the part of Great Britain.
Here it was again refolved to profecute the conqueft of France ; in confequence of which, the
former manifefto of Prince Cobourg was with-
drawn ; and, agreeable to this refolution, a new
manifefto, in terms very different from the for-

mer, was, on the day following, publithed by that
general.

Thefe are facts which proclaim the intention of
parties, in a manner lefs ambiguous, and more forcible, than can be done by mere verbal declarations.

Another inftance of a fimilar nature occurs in
the tranfactions relative to the capture of Toulon.
As it was thought of great importance that the
Englith forces fhould be admitted into that place,
an agreement was made with the inhabitants, conformable to what appeared, at the time, to be
their prevailing inclinations. Let us hear the
proclamation of Lord Hood upon that fubject,
dated 28th Auguft 1793, when he obtained poffeffion of Toulon.

" Whereas the Sections of Toulon have, by
" their commiffioners to me, made a folemn de-
" claration in favour of Monarchy ; have pro-
" claimed Louis the XVII. fon of the late Louis
" the XVI. their lawful king ; and have fworn
" to acknowledge him, and no longer fuffer the
" defpotifm of the tyrants which at this time go-
" vern France, but will do their utmoft to efta-
" blifh monarchy, *as accepted by their late fove-*
" *reign in* 1789, and reftore peace to their dif-
" tracted and calamitous country ; I do hereby
" repeat, what I have already declared to the
" people of the fouth of France, that I take pof-
" feffion of Toulon, and hold it in truft only for
" Louis the XVII. until peace fhall be re-efta-

" blifhed in France, which I hope and truft will
" be foon."

After obtaining poffeffion of that place, however, and weighing the matter more fully, a declaration, in fomewhat a different ftrain, was fent
by his Majefty's command, to the commanders of
his fleets and armies employed againft France,
and to his minifters employed at foreign courts,
dated 29th October 1793. It is there faid, that
" his Majefty by no means difputes the right of
" France to reform its laws."—And afterwards
it goes on as follows : " The King demands that
" fome legitimate and ftable government fhould
" be eftablifhed, founded on the acknowledged
" principles of univerfal juftice, and capable of
" maintaining with other powers the accuftomed
" relations of union and of peace. His Majefty
" wifhes ardently to be enabled to treat for the
" re-eftablifhment of general tranquillity with
" fuch a government, exercifing a legal and per-
" manent authority, and poffeffing power to en-
" force the obfervance of its engagements. The
" King would propofe none other than equit-
" able and moderate conditions; not fuch as the
" expences, the rifk, and the facrifices of the war
" might juftify, but fuch as his Majefty thinks
" himfelf under the indifpenfible neceffity of re-
" quiring with a view to thefe confiderations, and
" ftill more to that of his own fecurity and of the
" future tranquillity of Europe."—And referring
to the calamities and diforders prevailing in that

country, " It is then in order to deliver them-
" felves from this unheard-of oppreffion, to put
" an end to a fyftem of unparalleled crimes, and
" to reftore at length tranquillity to France, and
" fecurity to all Europe, that his Majefty invites
" the co-operation of the people of France. It
" is for thefe objects that he calls upon them to
" join the ftandard of an hereditary monarchy,
" not for the purpofe of deciding, in this moment
" of diforder, calamity, and public danger, on all
" the modifications of which this form of go-
" vernment may hereafter be fufceptible ; but in
" order to unite themfelves once more under the
" empire of law, of morality, and of religion," &c.

In fhort, the inhabitants of France, inftead of
the conftitution 1789, promifed them by Lord
Hood, and upon the faith of which they had delivered Toulon into the hands of the Englifh, are
referred to fuch a government as they themfelves,
at the termination of the war, might frame under
the direction of England, with whom, at the fame
time, they were then to fettle the account of expences. This requires no comment. Had we, in
confequence of this tranfaction, or by whatever
means, been finally victorious, we fhould have procured a government to our liking in France, with
as much eafe as the French have lately done in
Holland.

But though there can be no doubt that the
combined powers intended to conquer France, we
are not fo certain that they intended to conquer

it for the benefit of the Bourbon family. It has
been afferted that the treaty of Pilnitz propofed
to difmember that country ; and the behaviour of
the Allies, in the hour of their fuccefs, tends to
confirm that affertion. When Valenciennes fur-
rendered to the Duke of York, his Royal High-
nefs took poffeffion of that place, not for the benefit of Louis the XVII. but *in behalf of the
Emperor of Germany*. Generous and wife adminiftrators of Britain ! Happy people, under the
aufpicious direction of fuch able and prudent Minifters ! ! ! With what a laudable fpirit have we
fpent our blood and treafure for the benefit of fo
firm, fo ufeful, and fo difinterefted an ally ! May
we not expect alfo, in the partition of that vaft
and fertile country, to obtain, for our fhare, a few
towns or diftricts, the maintenance and government of which will improve our economy, as the
revenue to be drawn from thence will contribute
to difcharge our national debt, and to alleviate
our burdens ?

Our fuccefs, however, was but of fhort duration ; and we have now experienced almoft three
years of uninterrupted defeat and difafter. During
this long period, the moft remarkable circumftance
has been that inflexible obftinacy with which our
Miniftry have perfevered in the primitive object
of the war. They feem to have thought, that
　　　——to be weak is miferable,
　　Doing or fuffering——
Their behaviour puts one in mind of the warrior in

Ariofto, who does not obferve that his head has
been cut off, but continues fighting as if nothing
had happened to him. This immoveable intrepidity has been moft confpicuous in that branch of
adminiftration containing the deferters from the
ancient Whigs, among whom no change of countenance, no voice, or geflure, unbecoming their
former profeffions, has hitherto been obfervable.
A late Lord Lieutenant has, even recently, in a
public debate, recommended our perfeverance in
the conqueft of France, with a warmth that does
great honour to the fincerity of his feelings ; and
old Truepenny, it is faid, repofing upon his pen-
fions, ftill fwears againft a *regicide peace*.

Our Prime Minifter, indeed, has been brought
to admit, that the form of government in France
prefents no infuperable objection to our concluding
a peace with that nation ; an admiffion which appears to have been extorted, not without fome wry
faces, and much hefitation ; and which, after all
his vain boafting, was, doubtlefs, to him, if that
were of any importance, abundantly humiliating.
But this declaration feems to produce no alteration in his meafures; and peace is apparently as
remote as ever. What is now his object in continuing the war, the Lord only knows. But if any
fagacious projector could, in our very critical fituation, hit upon the plan of a peace, which would
not threaten to drive our prefent Minifters from
the poffeffion of their places, it is probable he
would meet with due encouragement. I am, &c.

CRITO.

LETTER XII.

TO THE EDITOR OF THE SCOTS CHRONICLE.

SIR,   Auguſt 16. 1796.

AFTER examining the real, and the pretended objects of the war, as well as the reaſons which have been given for inducing the nation to engage in it, I cannot forbear adding a few remarks, concerning the *injuſtice*, and concerning the *impolicy* of that undertaking. With reſpect to its *injuſtice* I ſhall ſay but little ; becauſe I am ſenſible that juſtice is too apt to be little regarded in the diſputes between different nations.

It ſeems to be univerſally admitted by writers upon the law of nature, and, ſo far as I can obſerve, is not diſputed by our miniſters themſelves, that every independent ſtate has an excluſive right to legiſlate for itſelf, and to ſettle its own internal government. This is a principle which makes its way directly to the underſtanding, and to the feelings of every enlightened mind. It is ſupported, not only by the immediate ſenſe of juſtice, but by the cleareſt and ſtrongeſt conſiderations of expediency. Every nation is beſt acquainted with its own peculiar circumſtances, and having invariably its own intereſt in view, is the beſt qualified to judge of thoſe meaſures by which its welfare is likely to be promoted. But the intereſt and views of different nations are always different, and frequently oppoſite to one another ; and if a foreign ſtate were

permitted to interfere in making laws, or framing
a conſtitution for its neighbours, there can be no
doubt that it would, in ſuch caſes, be directed by
very improper motives ; that the advancement of
its own power or emolument would often be the
real object ; and that the happineſs or proſperity
of the nation for whom it acted would be merely
a pretence. To allow ſuch interference, therefore, would be to ſacrifice the welfare, and even
ſometimes the exiſtence, of one independent ſtate,
to the caprice, the ambition, or the avarice of its
neighbours ; to afford a perpetual colour and pretext for invaſion and oppreſſion ; and to give an
open and regular licenſe to anarchy, rebellion, rob-
bery, and murder.

That, in the conduct of nations, this principle
has frequently been violated, and that powerful
ſtates have, in many caſes, produced revolutions
in the conſtitution of their weaker neighbours, upon pretence of conſulting the general intereſt or
ſafety, is a melancholy truth. We may mention,
as one inſtance of ſuch an attempt, in our own
country, the *partition treaty*, planned by King
William, but which, being diſapproved of by the
great and good Lord Somers, or from whatever
cauſes, was never carried into execution ; and as
another, the war about the ſucceſſion to the crown
of Spain, which took place at the beginning of the
preſent century. But the frequency of ſuch violations of the rules of juſtice only ſhows, that great
bodies of men, where multitudes act in concert

with each other, have lefs fenfibility to the feelings of morality than private and unconnected individuals. The number of perfons embarked in the fame undertaking, and actuated by the fame paffions, keep one another in countenance ; they meet with nobody that is cool and impartial, to cenfure their conduct, or to reprefent its enormity and bafenefs; and having in view a common intereft among themfelves, they appear to act, in part at leaft, not from felfifh motives, but from a fort of benevolence or public fpirit. This obfervation, however, though it may explain, is very far from being intended to vindicate fuch proceedings.

The attempts to juftify the war with France appear to have refted upon two different grounds, which are, in reality, incompatible with each other. Firft, it has been pretended, that we entered into that war from abfolute neceffity, the French having declared hoftilities againft us ; or, at leaft, that we acted merely upon the defenfive, having had no other means of preventing the progrefs of their arms. This view, which reprefents the prefent conteft as founded upon fimilar grounds to thofe which have produced the greater part of quarrels among nations, I had formerly occafion to examine, in ftating the reafons which were alleged for our engaging in the war; and to add any thing further upon it would be fuperfluous. Though the French made the firft verbal declaration of war, yet our behaviour had previoufly been fully equivalent to an actual declaration of hoftili-

ties. It is, at the fame time, well known, that the
Britifh miniftry avowed their purpofe of profecuting the conteft upon other grounds than that of
felf-defence; that France had both an intereft and
an inclination to maintain a good underftanding
with Britain ;. and that fhe made feveral attempts
to terminate the difpute by an amicable negociation.

I fhall at prefent confider the conteft in its peculiar, and true light ; as a war founded upon a
determined purpofe to interfere in the internal government of France, to pull down that conftitution
which the people themfelves had eftablifhed, and
to reftore an order and fyftem of policy which the
people, by an almoft unanimous confent, had reprobated.

This interference, the fupporters of the war
have endeavoured to vindicate upon two different
principles. It has been faid, in the firft place,
that Britain, from a regard to the French themfelves, and to the general interefts of human nature, had a right to interfere in the internal policy
of France, to defend the rights of the fovereign,
and thofe of the emigrants, to put a ftop to the
cruelties and to the anarchy prevailing in the
country, to affume the guardianfhip of the Chriftian religion, and of the rules of morality, which
were openly exploded, and treated with every
mark of fcorn and indignity.

The queftion is, whether we are entitled to new-
model the government or policy of a neighbour-

G

ing nation from pretences of this nature ? From
what I formerly obferved, it muft be evident, that
the permiffion of fuch interference would open a
door to much worfe evils than thofe which we
fhould propofe to redrefs. The pretence of generous, humane, or virtuous motives, would always
be at hand to cover fecret and unwarrantable defigns. The majority of an independent ftate will
commonly act with propriety in promoting their
own intereft ; or if, in a fingular emergency, they
fhould happen to do otherwife, they are likely
foon to correct their miftakes, and to rectify their
conduct. But the interpofition of foreigners, by a
military force, inftead of removing, is moft likely
to aggravate the diforders which have been committed. Can any thing be more abfurd than for
Great Britain to imagine that, by means of her
fleets and armies, fhe is capable of maintaining in
France the virtues of humanity and benevolence,
or of enforcing the principles of morality and the
Chriftian religion ? Does any perfon believe, that,
by attempting to do fo, fhe would not produce
more harm than good ?

But in reality the evils complained of in France
have arifen, at leaft in a great meafure, not fo
much from the fault of the French themfelves, as
from the conduct of Britain and her allies. Had
it not been for the Treaty of Pilnitz, and its confequences, there would have been no fuch diforders in that country. The limited monarchy,
eftablifhed in 1789, would have remained ; the

lives of the Sovereign, and of the Royal Family,
would have been preferved ; the bloodfhed, in ac-
complifhing fo great a revolution, would have
been wonderfully little ; and there would have
been no emigrants but fuch as voluntarily abandoned their native country rather than fubmit to
the new conftitution. We refemble a phyfician,
therefore, who having previoufly adminiftered a
poifonous drug to occafion a violent difeafe, kindly
offers his beft endeavours in curing the patient ;
and who, inftead of waiting till he is called for
that purpofe, endeavours, as in fome German
farces, to feize the unhappy fufferer, and follows
him from place to place, attempting in vain to
force his medicine upon him. ·

The other ground, upon which we have pretended to the right of overturning the prefent government of France, is a regard to our own intereft ; and in this we are probably more fincere.
The interefted fupporters of the abufes in our own
goverment pretend, and our honeft well-meaning
alarmifts appear to be convinced, that our own
political fyftem is endangered by the French Revolution.

It is certain that the late changes in the government of France have had a tendency to excite, in
this ifland, as well as over all Europe, an attention
to the general principles of government, and a difpofition to refcue mankind from flavery and oppreffion. I fhall even admit, for the fake of argument, that the example of a republican fyftem in

G ij

France may have some effect upon the inhabitants of this, and of other countries, in recommending to them that form of government: But will any person take upon him to assert, that the hazard arising from thence to Great Britain is of such magnitude, or so direct and immediate, as to justify our interference, by force, to overturn or alter the internal government of France? Does the establishment of a republic in France, together with the enthusiastic spirit which prevails among the people, threaten the government of this country with such immediate destruction as to excuse our violating the ordinary rules of justice, and invading our neighbours upon the mere principle of indispensible self-preservation? According to this mode of reasoning, every country in the world would be entitled to quarrel with its neighbours for establishing among themselves a different political system. Louis XIV. acted meritoriously in his attempts to conquer Holland, where a republican government was established; most divinely, in supporting the two rebellions against the House of Hanover, by whose accession we, in this country, were secured in a limited monarchy, very adverse to the despotism in France. The King of Prussia, and the Empress of Russia, who have lately crushed in the bud the liberties of Poland, are two angels sent from heaven, to prevent the progress of political innovation, and to defend mankind from the pernicious attempts of republicans and levellers.

Citizens of Britain, know your own good fortune, and learn to prize the ineftimable bleffings
of that Conftitution which has been handed down
by your forefathers. Are you in earneft in wifhing to preferve it to the lateft pofterity ? Be affured, that force and violence are not the proper
means for effecting this important purpofe. This
purpofe is not to be effected, either by attempting
to overthrow the political fyftem of your neighbours, or by punifhing with immoderate feverity
fuch of your countrymen as take the liberty of
cenfuring your own; but by mending your own
Conftitution where it is defective, by fubmitting it
with full confidence to the free examination of all
the world, and by conducting its adminiftration in
fuch a manner as, inftead of marking jealoufy and
diftruft, or infpiring difcontent and refentment,
will conciliate the love and affection, the lively
gratitude and zealous attachment of the people.
The Britifh-Conftitution is an old fabric, ftrong,
maffy, and well contrived, equally fitted to defend
againft the winter ftorm and the fummer's heat.
It would furely be madnefs, as well as the groffeft
injuftice, to demolifh the more fplendid or fafhion-
able houfe of your neighbour, left by its new-
fangled ornaments it fhould put you out of conceit with your own; but found reafon fhould teach
you, as foon as poffible, to repair the injuries
which time and accidents have occafioned to your
own building. Covet not the frippery of modern
embellifhments, the fancied improvements of fpe-

culative architects ; but let the reparation be exe-
cuted in that ftyle of plainnefs and fimplicity which
is agreeable to the original plan ; beftowing upon
it, at the fame time, all the accommodation, all the
free intercourfe of apartments, all the light and
cheerfulnefs of which that plan is fufceptible.   If
you act in this reafonable and liberal manner,
there is no ground to fear that this venerable pile
will ever be thrown down by its inhabitants, or
that its houfehold gods will ever be deferted.

To conclude, with refpect to the injuftice of the
war, I wifh I could avoid remarking, that the
weight of this charge lies chiefly upon us.   We
were not, indeed, the firft to invade France ; but
we took arms whenever we faw that the country
could not be conquered without our affiftance ;
and we foon became the leaders and directors of
the undertaking.   We over-perfuaded Holland
to take a fhare in the conteft ; we fubfidifed Sardinia ; we fubfidifed Pruffia ; we did what is equivalent to fubfidifing the Emperor.   Whatever
was the object of our miniftry in the beginning,
they have fince purfued it with an inflexible refolution, which no change of circumftances, no motives of national intereft or fafety, have been able
to flacken or divert.   After a long and inceffant
accumulation of difappointment, mortification, and
calamity, they continue, like the animal in the
fable, to gnaw the file, miftaking or mifreprefenting
the blood that appears for that of their enemies.
Not contented with becoming the prime mover

and foul of the combination againft France, they
have tried to force into the confederacy thofe few
powers of Europe who had refolved to maintain a
neutrality. The operations of our ambaffador at
Copenhagen, of Mr. Drake, our envoy at Genoa,
and of Lord Hervey, our envoy at Florence, are
fufficiently known. The Genoefe refifted the
rough attacks that were made upon them with a
degree of fpirit, which, from fo inconfiderable a
ftate, could hardly have been expected. The
Grand Duke of Tufcany, much againft his interest
and his opinion, found it neceffary to yield, and to
declare hoftilities againft the common enemy.
Upon what principle of morality they ventured to
treat independent ftates in this manner, it is not
eafy to fay. The barbarity of compelling a fovereign to involve his fubjects in all the miferies and
calamities of war, and this in oppofition to his own
fenfe of right and wrong, in fomething that out-
rages the feelings of juftice in a very uncommon
degree. I am, &c.

CRITO.

LETTER XIII.

TO THE EDITOR OF THE SCOTS CHRONICLE.

SIR, Auguft 23. 1796.

CONCERNING the *impolicy* of the war, there
occur fo many remarks which prefs forward and
feem to merit attention, that I am afraid of wan-

dering in a boundlefs field, and of encroaching too far upon the important information ufually collected in your very intelligent paper. To form a juft opinion upon the fubject, it would be neceffary to examine the following particulars :—

1. Whether the conqueft of France was a meafure calculated to procure the object which we had in view.

2. How far we were likely to fucceed in the project of conquering France.

3. What might be the probable confequences of our complete fuccefs in that meafure.

4. The inconveniences and mifchiefs to which we unavoidably expofed ourfelves by that undertaking.

The firft article abovementioned has been already confidered at fome length, in examining the caufes of the war; and I. fhall not trouble you with a repetition of the obfervations formerly made. The intention of our minifters in attempting the conqueft of France was to ftop the progrefs of what are called French opinions. The crufades, for the purpofe of redeeming the holy fepulchre from the hands of infidels, were not half fo abfurd; for thofe expeditions had really fome tendency to procure the ridiculous end which was propofed. But the cudgelling twenty-five millions of people out of a fyftem of opinions, which they had moft deliberately adopted, and which they confidered as effential to the fecurity of their lives and their property, is evidently beyond the reach of human ſtrength. Had we marched our victorious armies from one corner of France to the other, had we ſubverted all the new inſtitutions, and reſtored the old government in France, had we broiled ten thouſand Jacobins at a Britiſh *auto da fe*, we ſhould probably have been as far as ever from our purpoſe, either of ex-tinguiſhing republican tenets in that country, or of perſuading the people in this iſland, that a re-form of parliamentary repreſentation is not indiſ-penſibly requiſite for the preſervation of their li-berties.

But ſuppoſing that the conqueſt of France would have extirpated theſe offenſive opinions, it was a wide ſtep to conclude that this could be accom-pliſhed by the joint efforts of thoſe potentates who had formed a combination againſt her. Did thoſe potentates conſider the populouſneſs, the fertility, and riches of France; the compactneſs of her do-minions, her military ſpirit, and her ſuperiority in the military ſcience, particularly in that branch which relates to the management of artillery, now become the chief inſtrument of modern tactics? Were they aware that a nation, in thoſe circum-ſtances, comprehending near a fourth part of the inhabitants of Europe, could ſend greater armies to their frontiers, at leaſt armies which, when fighting for every thing that is dear to them, would do more execution than thoſe which all Europe, in the view of a foreign conqueſt, could maintain at a diſtance? Did they take into the

account the many fortified towns belonging to
France, on that fide where alone fhe is expofed to
an enemy, and which the late King of Pruffia,
from whofe opinion, in matters of this kind, our
lawyer minifters, or parliamentary orators might
not be afhamed to reap inftruction, confidered as
an impregnable defence? " The frontiers of
France next to Germany," fays that great military genius, " are like the jaws of a lion, with two
dreadful rows of teeth, ready open to devour any
invader."

But whatever obftacles to the conqueft of France
might occur in ordinary cafes, thefe are greatly
multiplied on the prefent occafion. France, as
our minifter himfelf acknowledged, has now become an ARMED NATION, capable, by a fimple re-
quifition, of bringing into the field fuch multitudes
as refemble the fwarms which, in a rude ftate of
fociety, iffued from the northern parts of Europe,
to overwhelm the provinces of the Roman Empire ; and thefe multitudes, animated by an enthu-
fiaftic love of liberty, which, added to their difcipline and military fpirit, appears to render them
invincible. The effects of that enthufiafm, joined
to that military fpirit and difcipline, we had fully
experienced in the total difcomfiture of the
Duke of Brunfwick ; in the rapid conqueft of the
Auftrian Netherlands ; and in the decifive battle
of Jemappe. That any perfon of found mind, after fo impreffive a trial, fhould have propofed to
renew the project of conquering that country, was

not to be expected. It exceeds the castle-building of a dream, or the delirium of a fever. We had seen the unanimity with which the French nation reprobated our designs in favour of monarchy; and if we trusted to the divisions in that country, and to the ferment of political factions, we took the infallible method of precluding any advantage from that source, by uniting every party against the common enemy of all. We became the Sir Martin Mar-all in the great theatre of Europe; and stumbled upon the very measure which excluded the possibility of our ever attaining the object of our wishes.

But supposing that, in spite of every obstacle, we should, by some miraculous interposition, have been successful in conquering France, may it not reasonably be demanded, what national advantage could possibly have resulted from that conquest? Was it proposed that, after we had restored the ancient despotism, and replaced the emigrants in their former situation, we should leave the French monarchy, thus happily renovated, to go on in its natural channel. Some additional precautions, I am afraid, would have been requisite for securing the continuance of our workmanship. We must, undoubtedly, have left in the country an army, and a great one too, for supporting that system of government which we had established, and for preventing an enraged and desperate people from cutting the throats of those detested rulers whom we had set over them. An English mercenary army,

of fufficient magnitude, and properly trained up in
the pleafant fervice of keeping the French demo-
crates in fubjection, would form an excellent corps
to be entrufted with the guardianfhip of Englifh
liberty; and would, in all probability, be often
appealed to in any of thofe future difputes, in England, which might arife between the crown and
the people.

But it is poffible that our governing politicians,
intoxicated with power, might pleafe themfelves
with the profpect of depreffing ftill more our ancient rivals, and might prefer the project of dif-
membering the French monarchy. Would Britain, in that cafe, have chofen to retain any part
of it? Would Britain, who finds the expence of
holding the infulated rock of Gibraltar fo infup-
portable, have fubjected herfelf to the burthen of
maintaining a number of garrifoned towns in France,
and to the hazard of being involved, as a principal
party, in all the wars of the Continent? To avoid
thefe evils, would we have chofen to leave this
contefted country in the poffeffion of our allies, to
be divided by them, like Poland, or to be difpofed
of as they, in their great humanity and juftice,
fhould pleafe to determine?

We could, in that cafe, indeed, have no fecurity
that the powers, whom we had thus aggrandized
beyond meafure, would not proceed, in a fhort
time, to the partition, or conqueft of Britain,
whofe commerce they have long envied, and whofe
government they cannot fail to deteft.

To whatever fide we turn ourfelves, in whatever
light we view this project of conquering France,
it appears no lefs pregnant with danger and calamity than it is abfurd and chimerical ; and fo far
is it from prefenting any folid profpect of national
benefit, that the mifchiefs to be apprehended from
our final fuccefs would be infinitely greater, and
more fatal, than even thofe which we have fuffered, and are likely to fuffer, by our complete fail-
ure and difappointment.

In eftimating, however, the folly and madnefs
of this infatuated project, we muft not overlook
the national advantages which have been forfeited,
or the inconveniences, the loffes, and the mifchiefs
which we have reafon to expect ; and which (for
unhappily we need not here depend upon conjec-
ture) we have actually fuftained from it. Of the
multitudes *killed off* in the courfe of the war,
which are much greater than we ever had, or ever
fhall have any account of, I will fay nothing ; for
Minifters appear to reckon it a prefcriptive privilege to facrifice as many lives as they pleafe to
their ambition or private emolument. But the
age in which we live is faid to be the age of cal-
culators. Let me afk our arithmeticians, what
fums of money have been loft ? What was the
amount of that alarming ftagnation of trade, which
began upon the commencement of the war, and
which made it neceffary that government fhould
fupport the credit of merchants by extenfive loans
of public money ; an interpofition calculated to

H

bring the mercantile intereſt under the immediate influence of the executive power? What is the amount of thoſe depredations upon our ſhipping, which have ſo raiſed the price of inſurance, and ſo impaired and clogged our foreign trade? What is the amount of the danger, to which we are now expoſed, of being excluded from foreign harbours, and of having our merchandize captured in neutral bottoms? But above all, what is the amount of that public 'expenditure which the war has occaſioned? Has it not been affirmed, upon good authority, that our public debt is already augmented by an hundred millions; and that the demands upon the Treaſury are pouring in from all quarters, with ſuch rapidity, that a new loan, to a great extent, will be neceſſary for the preſent year? It is computed that, though we ſhould be fortunate enough to conclude a peace with the utmoſt expedition, our national debt will be ſo enormous as to require a conſtant annual revenue of three or four-and-twenty millions; a ſum, by the miniſter's own confeſſion, fully equal to the landed rent of the kingdom. What a proſpect does this open to the future commerce of Britain, clogged with ſuch a weight of taxes? What a proſpect does it open to the landed intereſt, who, according to ſome ſyſtems of political economy, ſuſtain the whole of this burden, but according to all, muſt bear a great proportion of it? What a proſpect does this open to annuitants, and to ſuch as live upon a yearly ſalary or ſtipend, whoſe real fund of ſubſiſtence, af-

ter deducting the taxes which are paid from it, is
reduced to a mere trifle, while the price of all
commodities must, from the same cause, be in proportion augmented? But where will this end?
Will this bubble continue to swell for ever without bursting?

How different would have been the aspect of
our affairs, had we, during the conflict of the con-
tinental powers, remained in a state of neutrality?
Had we, indeed, used our endeavours, we might
easily have prevented the war altogether. But
supposing the struggle to have been limited to the
Continent, we should have carried on, without im-
pediment, all the trade of Europe, and its depen-
dencies; and the commerce of all other nations
would have been sheltered under our wings. In-
stead of adding to our public debts, the increase
of our wealth, and our resources, would have enabled us in proportion to extinguish our former
burdens. Without engaging in hostilities, we
might have put ourselves in a state of preparation
for our own defence; and by retaining our own
strength unimpaired, we might have expected,
that, after the contending parties had mutually
exhausted themselves, we should become the arbi-
ters of their pacification.

The mischiefs arising from the war, which re-
late more immediately to our government and po-
lice; that immense military force which, in different shapes, and by new and unprecedented insti-
tutions, has been spread over the country; the

H ij

meafures that have been purfued for feparating the
foldiery from the reft of the inhabitants ; the fevere punifhments, unfuitable to a polifhed nation,
which have been inflicted on political offences ;
the unufual and dangerous powers committed to
adminiftration ; the fufpenfion of the great bul-
wark of our perfonal liberty ; the unconftitutional
reftrictions which have been laid upon the intercourfe of the people, in examining their grievances,
and in petitioning for redrefs ; thefe, and fuch o-
ther political effects of the war, I fhall not at prefent enter upon. Here let me drop the curtain ;
leaving behind the fcene tranfactions which are
not neceffary for proving the point I had in view,
and the full exhibition of which would be too fevere a tax upon your indulgence and good humour.

I am, &c.

CRITO.

LETTER XIV.

TO THE EDITOR OF THE SCOTS CHRONICLE.

SIR,   September 2. 1796.

After the reflections which have been fug-
gefted concerning the impolicy of the war, I fhall
make no apology for confidering a little more particularly the fituation to which it has reduced us,
and the means moft likely to deliver us from the
difficulties and dangers with which we appear to
be furrounded. Our fituation is highly critical
and alarming. Our profpect is gloomy ; and the

clouds appear ftill to gather around us, without difcovering a rack, in any corner of the fky, to indicate the approach of funfhine and ferenity. We fet out, three years ago, in this unprofperous war, with high hopes and arrogant pretenfions. Our allies were numerous and powerful. We thought of no lefs than uniting all the ftates of Europe, whether great or fmall, againft the French Republic; and we expected to employ fuccefsfully the two great engines of *force* and *famine* for effecting our purpofes. What a dreadful reverfe of fortune have we fuftained! The Stadtholder, for whofe intereft we at firft pretended to commence hoftilities, is now an exile, ftripped of his dominions; and the Dutch, from being the enemies, are converted into the firm and zealous allies of the French. Spain and Pruffia are nearly in the fame fituation.. Ruffia fupports our caufe only by *declarations*; and the Emperor, after fhrinking into a mere auxiliary, dependent upon the pecuniary affiftance of Britain, is no longer able to hold up his head even in that fubordinate capacity, or to beftow that protection which is requifite for maintaining any authority or influence in the Germanic body. Sardinia, who, engaged in the war in confequence of a fubfidy from us, has, from abfolute neceffity, fubmitted to the law of the conquerer; and all Italy has, in the moft humble manner, petitioned for peace. So completely have the tables been turned, that France is now imitating the example we formerly fet them, by feizing our merchandize in the veffels of neutral nations; and is even threatening to exclude our foreign trade from thofe ports and markets to which it has hitherto been deftined. In fhort, we are evidently upon the point of being reduced to grapple alone with an enemy who has proved too powerful for almoft all Europe; and in this defperate conjuncture, we have reafon to fear that many of the neighbouring ftates will rejoice in feeing, or perhaps in promoting the downfall of a maritime power which they have long regarded with envy and jealoufy. What is now become of the big words of our minifter? What is become of his promife, that the French would not be able to continue their efforts for a month or a fortnight? What is become of his calculations founded upon the debafement of the affignats? His promifes, his predictions, his calculations, have all vanifhed in fmoke. In vain would he attempt any longer to impofe upon us. His fwelling tones can no longer be heard; his threatening afpect remains in the form of a ridiculous grimace; and he appears, like the counterfeit mufician in the play, continuing to move his fingers, in the fame order and method, after the mufic has completely ceafed.

The moft alarming circumftance, perhaps, in our prefent melancholy fituation, is that dejection and defpondency in which the nation appears to be funk, by the dangers with which fhe is threatened, and by the long train of mortification and difappointment which fhe has met with. Our faculties feem to be overwhelmed in a ftupid lethargy, which renders us incapable of any active exertion, and even of examining the extent of our misfortunes. Our politicians now hardly read the newfpapers, and are unwilling to fpeak of the public tranfactions. Have you heard any thing to-day? No! It feems to be all going the fame way! Need I obferve, that this feeble and cowardly fpirit is inconfiftent with the duty which, as faithful fubjects and good citizens, we owe to ourfelves, to our king, and to our country; and that its confequences, in all thefe different views, muft be equally ruinous. It is, indeed, the mere counterpart of thofe unprincipled and arrogant pretenfions which were fo lately exhibited. But in order to guard againft the impending evils, we muft look our danger in the face. We muft probe our wounds; we muft not fhrink at the appearance of the incifion knife, if it be neceffary to remove the malady which we have contracted.

If France fhall conclude a Peace with the Emperor, which is likely to happen very foon, there are *three* different ways by which that formidable enemy will probably endeavour to diftrefs Great Britain.

In the *firft* place, fhe will endeavour to exclude our commodities from all the foreign markets to which they have hitherto been carried. The effect of this meafure is faid to be already felt, in fome degree, by the French having taken poffeffion of Frankfort and Leghorn; and the reports,

in circulation, of their purfuing a fimilar policy
with refpeft to Hamburg and Lifbon, and even
with refpeft to the whole of the Baltic and Medi-
terranean, have become the fubject of univerfal
apprehenfion. That they will fucceed, to the full
extent of their views, in a project of·this nature,
I have no conception ; for as, according to the
proverb, *there is no friendſhip in trade*, fo we may
hold it equally certain that there is no *enmity*.
Merchants will trade with all the world, whether
friend or foe, wherever they find an advantageous
market. But though this difpofition will, in the
long-run, overcome every obftacle, it cannot be
fuppofed to operate all at once ; and a length of
time, doubtlefs, will be requifite for devifing proper expedients to evade thofe prohibitions and dif-
couragements with which our commerce is likely
to be encumbered.· The extent of the pecuniary
lofs which this may occafion can hardly be eftima-
ted ; becaufe it is impoffible to afcertain the effects of a fudden, though but a temporary inter-
ruption to the trade of our great mercantile com-
panies ; and becaufe the indirect methods, by
which only the trade can be continued, muft be
attended with different degrees of expence, which
will contribute more or lefs to diminifh the profits.

There is ground, *alfo*, to believe, that France,
when fhe has concluded a peace with the Emperor, will fend a great force to the Weft Indies,
and attempt to conquer the Britifh colonies in that
part of the globe. The diftance, and the extent

of our poſſeſſions, in that quarter, make it extremely difficult for us to guard them effectually ; and
the meaſure of proclaiming liberty to the Negroes,
which the French are ſaid to have already execut-
ed in St. Domingo, and which they probably will
extend to all the iſlands of which they acquire the
poſſeſſion, muſt hold out an encouragement to join
their ſtandard, which cannot fail to be of great
ſervice in promoting their deſigns. Whatever
may be the effects of this policy with reſpect to
the power of France in the Weſt Indies, there can
be no doubt of its tendency to annihilate the dominion of Great Britain, and to produce a total
change in the political ſtate and government of the
country, as well as in the condition of its inhabitants. To ſay the truth, if the conſequences of a
violent and ſanguinary conteſt could be avoided,
if the immediate deſtruction of lives, and of property, which is likely to occur in that part of the
world, could be prevented, I am diſpoſed to think
that the final iſſue of the revolution to be expected would not be ſo hurtful as may, at firſt view, be
apprehended. The total independence of thoſe
colonies, and their complete emancipation from
thoſe reſtrictions, in point of trade, to which they
have hitherto been ſubjected ; an event which
every perſon of diſcernment will conſider at no
great diſtance ; will in all probability be a change
highly advantageous, both to them, and to the ſe-
veral European nations with whom they have been
connected ; as, by a greater competition, it will

beſtow upon the former much greater encouragement, and a better direction to induſtry ; and will
furniſh the latter, in greater abundance, and at an
eaſier rate, with the different productions of the
Weſt Indies. The experience of the preſent age
has demonſtrated the abſurdity of many regula-
tions to which the commercial intercourſe of the
world had long been ſubjected, and which were
thought indiſpenſibly requiſite. It was apprehended, not many years ago, that the emancipation and
independence of our North American colonies
would give a mortal blow to the commerce of the
mother country ; whereas the trade of Britain never attained ſuch proſperity as it has enjoyed ſince
the accompliſhment of that great revolution.

Laſtly, It is probable that the French, when
they have no other enemy to cope with, will con-
centrate their force, and direct their principal
views to the invaſion of Britain, or of Ireland, or
of both together. That our fleets, notwithſtanding their great ſuperiority, being obliged to keep
in large bodies for the purpoſe of guarding againſt
any conſiderable defeat, or, from adverſe winds,
being occaſionally rendered incapable of acting, as
happened at the revolution 1688, may not be, at
all times, able to prevent the enemy from pouring
a multitude of troops upon different parts of a
coaſt ſo extenſive, and ſo near both to France and
Holland, there is too much reaſon to fear; and
though I am firmly perſuaded that ſuch a de-
ſcent would meet with no countenance or aſſiſt-

ance from the inhabitants of this country, and
that in the end it would be entirely unfuccefs-
ful, it is impoffible not to forefee numberlefs inconveniences and difafters, which an enterprize
of that nature is likely to produce, in an open
country, where mercantile tranfactions are fo numerous and complicated, and where the fhaking
of the public credit is apt to be attended with an
immediate convulfion. We fhould then, indeed,
have, in one refpect, the fame advantage over our
enemies which they formerly had over us. We
fhould act with the refolution and firmnefs of men
fighting in their own defence, and endeavouring
to maintain their independence. The great body
of the people, upon whom the chief ftrefs of the
conteft muft be devolved, would then have an opportunity of wiping off the afperfions which formerly were caft upon them ; of fhowing how far
the fufpicions entertained, concerning their politi-
tical fentiments, had any foundation ; and of refift-
ing thofe attempts to fubvert our conftitution,
which, from what we have lately feen in Holland,
and what we now fee in Lombardy, might with
too much reafon be expected.

In whatever light we regard our prefent circumftances, every perfon, who is not entirely di-
vefted of the capacity of reflection, will be convinced, that we ought, before it is too late, to make
every exertion for putting an end to this calamitous war. But the queftion is, how this can be ac-
complifhed ; fince the pretenfions of the French

will naturally rife in proportion to their aftonifh-
ing fuccefs; and confidering, that they probably
entertain a mortal refentment againft Britain, whom
they cannot fail to look upon as the chief author
and conductor of hoftilities profecuted with fuch
implacable animofity and rancour?

That we fhould accept of a *difhonourable* peace,
even in our difaftrous circumftances, I hope no
Britifh fubject, whofe opinion is worthy of the leaft
attention, will ever propofe. On the other hand,
that we fhould obtain an advantageous one, can
hardly be expected. For this we muft thank that
Miniftry, by whofe wretched policy in undertaking
the war, and by whofe incapacity in conducting
it, we have been brought into this perilous fituation. I am far from thinking, however, that the
French are not, as well as every reafonable man
in this country, defirous of terminating the war;
and that even, if proper means are employed, a
peace may not be procured upon reafonable terms.
The adminiftrators of that country, if they are
guided by found views of policy, cannot furely entertain a wifh to difmember the Britifh dominions,
or to infift upon fuch conditions as would hazard
that defperate effort which Britain is capable of
making in defence of her national exiftence. The
French miniftry may be fuppofed to have no farther aim than the obtaining of fuch a treaty as is
likely to be permanent, and as may be expected
to fecure their new conftitution againft any future
attempts, upon our part, to overturn it. The idea

of univerfal fraternization imputed to them, if ever it exifted, has probably been long fince abandoned as impracticable. It would be the height of madnefs to require that our government fhould be rendered exactly conformable to theirs; but they may reafonably, perhaps, demand, that we fhould give fome evidence of our entertaining fentiments which are not inimical to their conftitution; and that, for this purpofe, the authors of our late political meafures, thofe who have conducted the force of Britain in fuch a manner as to demonftrate an implacable hatred to the French Republic, fhould be inftantly difmiffed from the helm. Without fuch a change upon our part, it is impoffible that there fhould be the appearance of a fincere reconciliation; and the propofal of a peace could lead to nothing more than a temporary armiftice, to be broken as foon as Britain has recovered her exhaufted refources. Whoever talks of a peace, without this preliminary ftep, is a mere party man, the adherent of that miferable junto by whom the nation has been expofed to fuch dangers, and involved in fuch calamities.

In another letter, I fhall confider the expediency, or rather the abfolute neceffity of this change, from circumftances relating to the internal ftate and government of the country.

I am, &c.

CRITO.

I

LETTER XV.

SIR,

In my laſt letter I obſerved, that, if we
are in earneſt in wiſhing to conclude a peace, we
muſt make it appear that we are cordially recon-
ciled to the French nation; that our views are no
longer hoſtile to their Conſtitution; and that we
have no plan, at any future period, to act in concert with other powers in diſturbing or undermin-
ing its eſtabliſhment. Conſidering our behaviour
for ſome time paſt; conſidering that, of all the
European powers, we have appeared the moſt inveterate enemies of this Conſtitution, it cannot be
expected that our profeſſions, with regard to ſuch
a change of ſentiments, will gain any credit, un-
leſs they ſhall be accompanied with a total change
of Miniſtry, and, as far as the French are concern-
ed, with a total change of our political conduct.

But a change of miniſtry and of meaſures is not
more neceſſary for enabling us to conclude a peace
with France, than for ſecuring our own future
tranquillity, and for preſerving the principles of
the Britiſh Conſtitution. If the preſent Miniſtry
have ſhown, as they certainly have, a moſt inflexible reſolution to deſtroy the new form of government, and to reſtore the ancient deſpotiſm in
France; if there be good ground to believe, as
there undoubtedly is, that they have not really
abandoned this reſolution, but only give way to a

temporary neceſſity, and will take the firſt opportunity of reſuming their former meaſures, and of creating new diſturbances in purſuance of the old quarrel, it would be egregious folly in us to pay any regard to their profeſſions; and the height of imprudence to permit that they ſhould remain in ſituations where they may play over again the ſame ruinous game at our expence. It has, indeed, been always underſtood, and is conſidered as a maxim founded upon the nature of our government, that every unſuccefsful war ſhould produce a change of Miniſtry. As our Miniſters are in all caſes refponſible for their conduct, they ought to be ſo more eſpecially in the direction of a war, which, of all the meaſures in which they can engage, is the moſt pregnant with danger and calamity. From their fuccefs in the adventure, the nation, who can have no other criterion of their merit, muſt form a judgment of their integrity, or their capacity; and, if the iſſue is extremely unfortunate, they may often deferve puniſhment, but furely, in all caſes, muſt forfeit the truſt and confidence of the public. It would be an alarming circumſtance, if, contrary to this natural courſe of things, a ſet of war-miniſters, who by their mifconduct had produced a ſeries of public difaſters, and had brought the nation to the brink of a fatal precipice, were ſtill able to retain their offices, and to proceed in their career. It would ſhow that they were upheld, upon a deteſt-

able fyftem of favouritifm, and, by a fecret interference, threatening to fubvert the Conftitution.

The application of this remark to our prefent
critical fituation is hardly neceffary. There furely
never was a war more unprofperous than the prefent, undertaken from worfe motives, or carried
on in fuch a blundering manner. There never
was a war, to which the people were excited by
fuch a train of delufion and impofture, or in which
their hopes were, from time to time, buoyed up,
and their paffions enflamed, by fuch a feries of
mifreprefentations and falfehoods. If the Miniftry who planned and conducted this infatuated
enterprife fhall remain in power after the conclufion of fuch a peace as Britain, in her untoward
circumftances, muft be contented to accept, we
can have no doubt that there is at the bottom
fome peculiar caufe of fo extraordinary a phenomenon, which requires to be inveftigated ; fome
fecret malady, affecting the vitals of the Conftitution, for which a remedy cannot be too foon provided.

It is evident, that not only a change of Miniftry, but a total change of *meafures*, has become
indifpenfably requifite for the prefervation of our
liberties.

Whoever is acquainted with the principles of
our Conftitution, and confiders the nature of the
Revolution-fettlement, in 1688, will eafily perceive
that, from the courfe of public events, and from
the changes in the ftate of fociety, great alterations

have, fince that period, occurred in our political
fyftem. By that great tranfaction, the boundaries
of the prerogative were afcertained and fixed, in
fuch a manner as precluded all hazard from any of
thofe encroachments againft which the nation,
from paft experience, had been taught to provide.
From this time forward, a new order of things was
introduced. The Houfe of Commons, no longer
jealous of the Crown, became hearty and liberal
in granting fupplies; and the expenfive wars in
which the nation was involved, occafioned a rapid
increafe of taxes. Minifters, taking advantage of
the national fpirit, became proportionably daring
and rapacious; and when the expence of their
projects could not be defrayed within the year,
they ventured to borrow a capital, providing only
a fum for the annual difcharge of the intereft.
Thus the fyftem of *funding*, which from fmall be-
ginnings was gradually extended, and has rifen to
fuch a monftrous pitch, taught the nation to engage in military undertakings beyond their ftrength,
and rendered her familiar with an endlefs accumulation of public burthens.

It is unneceffary to obferve, that this augmenta-
tion of the public revenue, by creating a corre-
fpondent increafe of patronage, has produced an
extenfion of *influence*, pervading all the different
branches of adminiftration, and advancing without
end, like the fources from which it is derived.
The public revenue, immediately before the Revolution, amounted to about two millions. Sup-

pofing that the prefent war is terminated with all
poffible expedition, it is believed that our future
peace eftablifhment cannot be below twenty-four
millions.   It would not be difficult to fhow, did
the limits of the prefent letter admit of fuch a particular difcuffion, that this increafe of the public
revenue, during the period above mentioned, has
produced an extenfion of influence far exceeding
the proportion of that increafe.   But throwing
this confideration afide, it muft be acknowledged
that, by the immenfe patronage arifing from the
difpofal of fo much money ; not to mention the
church livings in the gift of the crown, the ap-
pointments of the Eaft India Company, under the
controul and direction of miniftry, with many
other offices and places of emolument in their nomination, none of which are included in the foregoing calculation of the public revenue, there is
produced an univerfal afcendancy in all the departments of government, which often lulls afleep
and palfies our fenfe of duty, holds in derifion all
pretences to public fpirit, and feems at length to
overbear and deftroy all oppofition.   With what
propriety the different powers of government are
diftributed and balanced, how beautiful the political machine may appear in theory, and with
what apparent nicety its various parts are adjufted
to one another, is of little importance, if our minifters fhall be poffeffed of a magical inftrument,
by which they may fecretly tamper with all its

operations, and controul or direct all its move-
ments!

It was this view of our political ftate which, in
the courfe of the American war, extorted the memorable declaration from the Houfe of Commons,
" that the influence of the Crown had increafed,
" was increafing, and ought to be diminifhed."
It was the fame view which, upon the conclufion
of that war, produced, among men of all ranks, a
very general attention to a circumftance of great
importance in the government, (though formerly
it had excited little concern or uneafinefs) the un-
equal reprefentation of the community in the
Houfe of Commons. While the fecret influence
of miniftry, from the limited ftate of the revenue,
was inconfiderable, this deviation from the original principles of our government, which, in a
courfe of time, had proceeded from various caufes,
was attended, perhaps, with no great inconveni-
ence; but, in confequence of the vaft extenfion
of minifterial patronage, it came neceffarily to be
regarded as a defect, of the utmoft magnitude, in
the conftitution of the legiflature.

Notwithftanding the prodigious progrefs of Minifterial influence and corruption, there ftill remained one check upon the conduct of every Adminiftration, which had always been confidered as the
great fafeguard of our liberties. Though the doctrine
of abfolute confidence in Minifters had been exalted to a wonderful pitch, and though their meafures could, in ordinary cafes, be carried into exe-

cution with nearly the fame facility as in the moſt
deſpotical government, it was always expected,
that, upon extraordinary occaſions, when thoſe
meaſures had become extremely unpopular, the
interpoſition of the Houſe of Commons, by a peti‧
tion to the Crown, would infallibly produce a
change of Miniſtry, and a conſequent change of
ſyſtem. This ultimate controul, it was thought,
might prove a terror to evil doers, and might pre‧
vent the executive power from ſhutting its ears to
the loud voice of the nation. But the tranſactions
in the year 1784 put an end to that expectation ;
and demonſtrated, that if ever the Crown, from a
ſingular concurrence of accidents, ſhould loſe a
majority in that Houſe, its Miniſters might ſafely
venture upon a diſſolution of Parliament as an in‧
fallible expedient for ſupporting their intereſt. A
great majority of the Commons being, in the pre‧
ſent ſtate of the repreſentation, returned by the
intereſt of a ſmall number of individuals, a diſſolu‧
tion of Parliament, as far as related to that Houſe,
was not, in reality, an appeal to the nation at
large, but, in a great meaſure, an appeal to ſuch
of the nobility and gentry as had acquired the di‧
rection of *rotten boroughs*, or of certain political‧
diſtricts. After this leading experiment, it be‧
came now evident to all the world, that a reform
in the mode of electing the national repreſentatives
was indiſpenſably requiſite, for counteracting the
effects of that great influence acquired by Mini‧

fters, and for maintaining the free exercife of thofe powers eftablifhed at the Revolution.

It was by exprefling great zeal in the purfuit of this object, and by profefling various opinions of a fimilar tendency, together with the poffeffion of a pompous and plaufible eloquence, that our Prime Minifter had acquired fuch popularity as rendered him, at the time alluded to, a neceffary ally to that collection of the adherents of prerogative which came to be placed at the helm. He continued, when in office, to make fome feeble and aukward attempts for promoting a parliamentary reform, but foon acquiefced in the negative which was given to that meafure, chiefly by his minifterial friends. How far he had been in earneft in thofe attempts became evident in 1792, when a motion for the fame purpofe was brought, from another quarter, under the confideration of Parliament, and countenanced by a fociety of gentlemen, whofe rank and character afforded a fufficient pledge of their good intentions; upon which occafion, this verfatile ftatefman not only oppofed the meafure with all the weight of minifterial intereft, but endeavoured to hold it up to the public as calculated to promote the defigns of republicans and levellers. It was, in fact, to difappoint the meafures propofed at that time, as I formerly obferved, that the war with France was undertaken. Had a temperate reform been then carried into execution, the fyftem of alarm, which has been fo artificially fpread over the kingdom,

would have been fuperfeded; this ruinous war,
with all its dreadful confequences, would have
been prevented; and the national profperity would
have rifen to a height without example in any former period.

But if it was, at that time, a meafure of fupreme
neceffity to counteract the tendency of minifterial
influence, by correcting the inequality of the national reprefentation, how much more fo muft it
appear at prefent; when, in confequence of the
war, that influence has been fo wonderfully extended; and when the terrors which were excited,
and the malignant fufpicions which were inftilled
into the minds of men, have contributed to arm
our minifters with fuch new and unprecedented
powers? What an implicit faith in thofe Minifters has been inculcated? With what an abfolute dominion over all ranks and orders of men
have they been invefted? What difcretionary
powers have been committed to them on pretence
of guarding the public fafety, though at the expence of perfonal liberty; and what abufes have
been made of thefe powers by the profecution and
oppreffive treatment of innocent perfons? What
reftraints have been impofed upon the liberty of
the prefs, that neceffary inftrument for checking the
encroachments of prerogative? What reftraints,
what prohibitions have been laid upon the meetings of the people for the defence of their privileges? In a mixed government like ours, is it not
the privilege of every Britifh fubject to petition

the Sovereign; to petition Parliament, whenever
he conceives his rights to be invaded ? Is not this
privilege fecured exprefsly by the *Bill of Rights,*
that facred and fundamental law of the kingdom ?
But how are men to know when encroachments
are made upon their rights; and how are they to
petition with any effect for redrefs, if they are
not allowed to meet and converfe together upon
political fubjects ? And with what fort of freedom
can they communicate their thoughts, and procure
mutual information, if they are liable to be filen-
ced, imprifoned, and punifhed, at the difcretion of
an officer, appointed by that very executive power
of whofe oppreffion they may have occafion to
complain ?

When a parliamentary reform was propofed, immediately before the commencement of the war,
the chief objection, which any perfon chofe to
avow, was founded upon a fufpicion that the people
would not be contented with an amendment of
the defects particularly fpecified, but, in imitation
of the French, were, in reality, defirous of a total revolution. It is hoped the experience we
have had, fince that period, of the temper and
moderation of the people in all parts of the ifland,
will be fufficient entirely to remove this objection,
and to fatisfy us that the lower orders are in general firmly attached to the Britifh Conftitution.
They have undergone a fevere fcrutiny. Their
conduct has been ftrictly watched. No political
offences, however trivial, have been overlooked.

No pains have been fpared to convict offenders ; and the law has not withheld her utmoft feverity from fuch as were convicted. Nor has the conduct of Adminiftration, with refpect to the populace, been of a conciliating nature. But notwithftanding the mortifying fufpicions which have been caft upon them, notwithftanding the neglect which their humble petitions in behalf of their favourite object have conftantly met with, notwithftanding the invidious diftinctions which have unneceffarily and injudicioufly been held up between them and the fuperior ranks, they have never been betrayed into violent or unconftitutional meafures ; they have never teftified any marks of refentment againft the ruling powers ; and, under the preffure of uncommon difficulties, even in procuring their daily bread, they have waited with patience the iffue of a war which they could not approve of, and againft which they had in vain remonftrated. Of the many who were capitally profecuted for political offences, all have been acquitted by the verdict of a Jury, except two obfcure perfons in Scotland, of whom the principal was a noted fpy, that had received a bribe upon the part of the Executive Government.

Upon the whole, if meafures are not fpeedily taken to procure a peace, and to avert the impending evils, it will be impoffible to entertain a doubt, that the national profperity and happinefs are facrificed to the power of the prefent Minifters, and to the advancement of that minifterial

influence and corruption which they have fo ftea-
dily and fuccefsfully cultivated.

It is now time, Sir, that I fhould conclude
thefe remarks, with exprefling my fincere gratitude for your politenefs in giving them fo indul-
ging a reception in your entertaining and ufeful
repofitory. I am not vain enough to think that I
was capable of throwing any light upon fubjeds
which have already been fo much canvaffed by
men of the greateft abilities; but I wifhed to
corred fome miftakes, and to remove fome prejudices, which frequently occur in perfons expofed
to the want of fufficient information; a misfortune
of which their fuperiors are fometimes difpofed
to take advantage.. If I have, in any degree,
fucceeded in this attempt, my intention is completely anfwered.—I am,

SIR,

.

Your much obliged humble fervant,

CRITO..